Holistic Divorce

Sh*t Happens, It's How You Deal With It That Counts

By

Sushma Kotecha

Legal Notice

© Copyright 2023 ©*sushmakotecha*

All rights reserved. The content contained within this book may not be reproduced, duplicated, or transmitted without direct written permission from the author or the publisher. Email requests to kevin@babystepspublishing.com

Under no circumstances will any blame or legal responsibility be held against the publisher, or author, for any damages, reparation, or monetary loss due to the information contained within this book, either directly or indirectly.

Legal Notice:

This book is copyright protected. It is only for personal use. You cannot amend, distribute, sell, use, quote, or paraphrase any part, or the content within this book, without the consent of the author or publisher.

Disclaimer Notice:

Please note the information contained within this document is for educational and entertainment purposes only. All effort has been executed to present accurate, up-to-date, reliable, complete information. No warranties of any kind are declared or implied. Readers acknowledge the author is not engaging in the rendering of legal, financial, medical, or professional advice. The content within this book has been derived from various sources. Please consult a licensed professional before attempting any techniques outlined in this book.

By reading this document, the reader agrees under no circumstances is the author responsible for any losses, direct or indirect, that are incurred as a result of the use of the information contained within this document, including, but not limited to, errors, omissions, or inaccuracies.

Published by *Babysteps Publishing Limited* All enquires to kevin@babystepspublishing.com

ISBN: 9798375808062

Contents

A word from the Author……………………………..1

About the Author……………………………………..5

Acknowledgments…………………………………..11

How to use this book……………………………...13

Introduction………………………………………….15

PART ONE: BRACING FOR THE STORM……19

CHAPTER 1: A FAMILY SEPARATED WITHOUT BEING DESTROYED………………...21

Divorce in the UK, in numbers…………………..22

What's a holistic approach to divorce?.................22

Why a holistic approach to divorce?....................24

Where the four states meet……………………….27

A technique for making permanent life decisions………………………………………………..29

Is the D-Word the right answer?..........................31

What "winning" in a separation case looks like…34

PART TWO: DURING THE SEPARATION - FROM WE TO ME………………………………..35

CHAPTER 2: ADMITTING THAT IT'S OVER..37

The overlapping phases of grief………………….37

Finding peace in the storm……………………….39

A healthy outlet for emotions........................43

Understanding your role as a spouse and as a parent..46

Fighting the temptation to get back with your ex..47

CHAPTER 3: DEALING WITH STRESS & ANXIETY..51

What's Divorce Stress Syndrome (DSS)?.......... 52

What does DDS feel like?................................. 52

How stress and anxiety manifests in our body and mind...53

Making good decisions when we're stressed......55

Managing triggers...56

Emotional meltdowns.......................................59

Where's this anger coming from?.......................62

Visualising cutting the marital bond................63

CHAPTER 4: MEDIATION...........................67

What is family mediation?................................68

What family mediation isn't..........................…70

The four core principles of mediation...............71

What mediators do and how they help…..........72

When mediation is unsuitable.........................74

An introduction to MIAMs.........................76

What are the exemptions?....................................78

Collaborative divorce................................79

What if you can't agree? Other dispute resolution options...81

CHAPTER 5: LITIGATION AS THE LAST RESORT..85

What litigation means in the context of divorce..86

Comparing mediation to litigation..................89

Comparing litigation to arbitration..................90

The challenge in turning a divorce into a legal event..91

When litigation is absolutely necessary............93

Preparing for Litigation.............................95

A litigated case often doesn't go to a full trial...102

CHAPTER 6: SHARING THE NEWS AND GETTING SUPPORT.................................105

When's the right time?...105

How to go about it..106

Telling the children that you're divorcing.........107

Telling family that you're divorcing...............111

Telling co-workers and mutual friends............112

How things will change............................114

CHAPTER 7: THE JOURNEY THROUGH SEPARATION FROM THE CHILD(REN)'S VIEW..119

What children need at any age........................119

How are infants and toddlers affected by divorce?..120

Divorce from a pre-schooler's and a school age child's perspective......................................121

Divorce from the teenager's perspective..........122

What they'll learn......................................123

Do they deserve to know the truth?...................125

When the children are used as pawns..............127

Guiding children to work through their emotions..128

Finding answers to the difficult questions in advance...130

CHAPTER 8: THE ARRANGEMENTS THAT HAVE TO BE MADE.............................135

The options for sorting out child arrangements..136

Deciding where the children will live and "the welfare checklist".................................... 137

Coming up with a contact schedule and parenting plan...138

Child maintenance...140

Letting the children know about the new arrangements..141

CHAPTER 9: ANTICIPATING CO-PARENTING CHALLENGES......................................143

Parental alienation....................................143

Holding a grudge against your ex..................146

Co-parenting with a narcissist.....................147

Competition between two parents.................149

Parallel parenting....................................150

CHAPTER 10: CO-PARENTING................153

What is co-parenting?..................................154

The benefits to children............................154

What are some of the challenges?..................155

Making it work......................................157

Collective decision making........................160

Diffusing high tension situations..................162

Co-parenting in public spaces.....................163

PART 3: AFTER THE DIVORCE - HEALING 165

CHAPTER 11: ADJUSTING TO THE NEW LIFE..167

What will it be like after the divorce?..............167

You're now the head of the household...........168

Loneliness...168

Parental burnout..169

Instilling discipline in your children...............170

You may not always know what is "right".......171

Overcoming the fear of saying "no"...............172

Adjusting to single parenthood.....................173

Adjusting to the 'I' frame of mind.................174

Watching out for stumbling blocks................175

CHAPTER 12: FINANCES........................179

Ending a shared financial life and "the section 25 factors"... 179

How to deal with the matrimonial home.........183

Understanding your new financial needs.........184

Moving on, financially, after a divorce...........186

CHAPTER 13: GRIEVING A BROKEN RELATIONSHIP....................................193

Why broken relationships are so painful.........193

Making healthy choices...........................195

Reclaiming your life..............................202

How can we learn to be responsible for our well-being...204

Finding closure to the pain of divorce...........207

CHAPTER 14: A SUPPORT SYSTEM.........209

It's OK seeking help..............................210

The benefits of a support system..................210

Reaching out to friends and family...............213

Seeking help from a therapist or a divorce coach..214

CHAPTER 15: SELF CARE....................……..217

What is self-care?..217

A positive mindset...............................……....218

How can we develop it?..................................218

Building the resilience necessary to withstand the emotional hurricane............................………..221

Taking care of your mental health while co-parenting..223

Spending time with loved ones...................225

Self compassion.................................………225

Mindfulness..……...226

How mindfulness helps when going through a divorce..228

Evaluating areas that need to change.............230

Healing after a divorce through Yoga……….. 230

Benefits of Yoga after a divorce..................232

Meditation.....................................……….....232

Grounding to Mother Nature......................235

CHAPTER 16: VISUALISING YOUR FUTURE……...237

What is visualisation?..238

How can we use it to cope after a divorce?........238

CHAPTER 17: MOVING ON TO NEW RELATIONSHIPS……………………………...243

When should you start dating after a divorce?... 243

Asking the real questions…………………….244

The trap in casual hookups……………………245

Putting it all together…………………….…..246

What's next?... 247

A Word From The Author

Did you know that the biggest increase in trends over time, according to the Children and Family Court Advisory and Support Service (CAFCASS), has been in private law Children Act proceedings?

CAFCASS worked with 97,098 children in private law proceedings in 2022/23. The percentage of children involved in private law proceedings increased from 64.9% in 2017/18 to 67.7% in 2022/23.

Isn't it worrying that lawyers and court proceedings are considered the first port of call for sorting out child arrangements rather than the parents finding out a way to work together?

The Rt.Hon. Sir Andrew McFarlane, President of the Family Division, strongly believes that the family judicial system should only be used where there's a case of significant domestic abuse or safeguarding and welfare issues that go to the heart of the child arrangements. I'm totally with him on this, and I'm sure that most of my counterparts will be too.

Divorce and separation should be approached with kindness, compassion, understanding, acceptance, no judgement and letting go of the past for the greater good of all impacted. Sometimes, parents get stuck in the rut of believing that "custody battles" are about who "wins" when in reality, it should be about finding a solution that everyone can live with and that works best for the children.

Children pick up on the tension and anger coming from their parents during a divorce and separation: fights over who gets the dog and/or the cat, who gets the house, and who pays for what. It must stop. I know that it's easy to say, but trust me, I have been there and worn the divorce t-shirt. Breaking up without negative energy and vibrations will be a lot easier for everyone to move on.

I'm writing this book for three reasons. First, I want to share with you a new approach to divorce. One that sees separation as a new birth and beginning rather than an all-out war. One that sees separation and divorce as an opportunity to learn and grow instead of being a tragedy. *Divorce isn't a tragedy; staying in an unhappy marriage is the tragedy.* I know how difficult and painful it can be to move on from a marriage that didn't work out, but I also know it can be done with a clean, clear and peaceful heart.

The second reason is that I want to give you a co-parenting approach that brings love, kindness and compassion to the world. One that sees co-parenting as a way of finding the happiness, joy and peace that a child deserves with their parents working together despite their differences and the divorce. I know how difficult it is to have a voice in a world where you are constantly told that "going to court is the best option."

So, I want this book to be about hope, faith and healing for those who need it. As Mahatma Gandhi stated:

"We but mirror the world. All the tendencies present in the outer world are to be found in the world of our body. If we could change ourselves, the tendencies in the world would also change. As a man changes his own nature, so does the attitude of the world change towards him. This is the divine mystery supreme. A wonderful thing it is and the source of our happiness. We need not wait to see what others do."

In a nutshell, this means - be the change you wish to see in the world, recognise and understand that happiness is an inside job that comes from within.

Finally, and I've saved the best for last, this will be your self-care guide to deal with the divorce. One that will help you come back to your true authentic self and see the bigger picture so that you can heal and move forward with your life in a healthier, happier way. By taking a holistic approach to divorce, you will learn how to become self-aware, especially regarding your mental and emotional health and how to work together with your ex-spouse to co-create the life you really want for you and your children.

During this emotional roller-coaster where you just don't know what is around the corner, having a way to care for yourself is essential. I will be writing this book mostly from the perspective of men and women who are married or in a civil partnership that are going through a separation and divorce, but I know that if you are going through a separation after a co-habiting relationship, this book will be equally helpful to you too, allowing you to move to a place of peace and acceptance. And then you can move on to co-parenting and creating a life that is great for everyone - parents, children, extended family members, friends and your cats and dogs too!

Please note that this book refers to universal holistic principles to support families worldwide through a family break up. However, any references to family law, the legal systems, policies, procedures and statistics are only applicable to England & Wales.

I truly wish this book inspires and empowers those facing a family breakup to look at things differently, with a new perspective to make choices and decisions that will serve them and their families better. Allowing everyone impacted by separation and divorce to lead happier, healthier and more fulfilled lives post-separation and divorce.

On a final note, it goes without saying, but the lawyer in me demands that I record it here: this book is for information and guidance purposes only and does not constitute legal or financial advice. Readers are recommended to take appropriate advice from professionals as and when necessary to support their decision-making process.

About The Author

Sushma Kotecha lives in the East Midlands, England, where she practiced family law for over 27 years, having qualified as a solicitor back in January 1994.

She dual qualified as a family mediator in April 2010 and gained accredited status (the gold badge of honour!) to facilitate all issues of family mediation (both children and financial) in December 2015 via the Family Mediation Council and continues to hold accredited status.

Sushma is passionate about people and enjoys being in a profession that allows her to help couples in conflict during one of the most traumatic and difficult periods in their lifetimes.

Throughout her career, Sushma has worked for various firms and gained invaluable experience and knowledge in dealing with a wide range of people who come from all walks of life. She has always been committed to a holistic and non-confrontational approach to resolving family disputes.

In March 2021, she took a leap of faith and made the decision to give up a successful career in family law to focus on her passion and calling to help couples in conflict resolve disputes out-of-court. Her aim is to encourage a more holistic approach to separation and divorce and promote mediation and other dispute resolution options as the first port of call where it is considered safe and suitable. This is a kinder, compassionate approach to separation and divorce that she wholeheartedly advocates.

Research shows that divorce and separation do not lead to childhood trauma; it is the parental conflict that has an adverse impact on the child's emotional and psychological well-being that causes trauma, and this is one of the top 10 Adverse Childhood Experiences (ACEs). Sushma wishes to protect children from this trauma and diminish parental conflict. It is her desire to empower and inspire separating couples to take stock of their circumstances, stay in control, out of court and make their own informed, mindful decisions hence the birth of 'Holistic Family Mediation' – an online private family mediation service launched on 1 July 2021. This evolved into 'Holistic Family Mediation & Coaching' in April 2023.

Sushma is a divorcee herself, and thus she fully empathises and understands just how painful and difficult it is to deal with a family breakup. However, she is of the firm belief that divorce does not have to be so bitter, toxic and twisted. On the contrary, with commitment and effort on both parties' sides, it can be amicable, kind and compassionate.

Her mission is to flip the script on divorce, with a view to having a positive impact on separating couples, their children and future generations. We all have a choice as to how we navigate these turbulent times. Sh*t happens; it's how you deal with it that counts!

Sushma is a graduate of *the 'Holistic Life Coach and Mind-Body Practitioner'* diploma and also offers holistic divorce coaching as an alternative service to those who prefer to work with her on a one-to-one basis.

There is a better solution for separating and divorcing couples than going straight off to court to sort out issues. Sushma has seen first-hand how the judicial system can destroy relationships. Seems like a contradiction, right? A family lawyer who says going to court is damaging relationships. Well, that's what happens when you take families through the court system: they lose hope, trust and faith in each other and in the judicial process.

The traditional court-based system is rooted in a hard-line, "win-lose" approach to divorce. It's about who gets the last word and who gets what assets and financial support. It's not about "hope", "faith", and "healing" your marriage with compassion and kindness. Sushma believes that if you're going through divorce or separation, there is a better way. And this is it!

Throughout her practice as a family mediator, Sushma has facilitated mediation for hundreds of separating couples struggling to come to terms with the end of their relationship and marriage. She's seen the heartaches and knows how hard it is for everyone involved - especially when you have children.

She also knows that co-parenting can be a challenge for everyone, and sometimes, no matter how much you love your child and know you must do your best to find a solution, you need support from someone who knows what you're going through. So, she wanted to write this book to inspire and empower those that find themselves in this situation to find a way out, to find peace of mind and a future to look forward to.

For her, a kinder, compassionate approach to separation and divorce means that everyone can move on to lead happier, healthier and more fulfilled lives post-separation and divorce, with a clean, clear heart and respect for each other.

Who is this book for?

1. Those looking for an alternative to the traditional, hard-line approach to divorce and separation where the court is the only solution

Conventionally, the divorce process was a linear, binary process involving the following:

A court case with a judge who hears both sides of the story and decides on what's best for your children and your family both in terms of the child and financial arrangements.

A lawyer who may or may not be empathetic to what you're going through and will likely want to argue either "for" or "against" their client's decision so that they can "win" their case.

While this approach works, it removes the human touch from the divorce process. And it doesn't help couples find a way to work together and move through the trauma of separation and divorce so that they can go on with their life. In fact, it does the opposite - it polarises the parties and fuels conflict and resentment.

2. The recently separated or divorced parent who needs help navigating and regulating his or her emotional status

The divorce process is made of three events, often happening simultaneously. There's the official legal side of your divorce, the emotional side of the separation and co-parenting, and then the more spiritual side of healing. Because these three events are combined as one single event, it's easy for you to get lost in your emotions and forget about the other elements of the divorce. This book can help you see the bigger picture of divorce and separation so that you can focus on what's really important at this time in your life.

3. Therapists and other professionals who want to understand the new ways of working with families

Therapists and professionals who support couples in conflict going through a divorce will learn what to expect during this process, how to talk about serious issues with parents for the best interests of their clients, and how to encourage those parents to be more open-minded when it comes to finding a solution that works for everyone.

By advocating for mediation and other dispute resolution options, this book can help therapists, and other professionals embrace the new paradigm of divorce and separation so that they can help parents get through the process in a much more positive and healthy way.

4. Divorcees who are healing on their own and want to take a proactive approach to lead a life that brings peace and joy

Sushma has seen how the divorce process can benefit from parents taking an approach that is proactive and emotionally intelligent. She believes that you can heal from your past and create a new life where you're living in the present with hope and faith for a brighter future.

She believes in taking an approach where you're mindful of your emotions, taking good care of yourself, and coming to balance with all aspects of your life. It's about building a new foundation for yourself that will work for you together with your ex-spouse.

5. Those who want or need a guide on how to work with your ex-spouse in a way that will bring fearlessness, love and courage into your life

Even after your marriage is officially over, if you have children together, your relationship with your ex-spouse isn't over. Your children need both of you to be happy and healthy, as do you.

So, if you want to create a life that works for everyone, then it's time to think outside the box. Sushma will guide you through this process by helping you focus on what really matters - your peace of mind, health, happiness and everything else that goes into creating the life that works for you and your family.

Acknowledgements

Firstly, I'd like to offer deep gratitude to my "inner circle" and acknowledge them for supporting me throughout my tough and challenging times. Without your unconditional love and unwavering support, I don't think I would have come so far or had the courage and strength to take the bold, brave steps that I have taken over the past several years to turn my life around. My inner circle are my beloved parents; Manu and Kanta, my wonderful maternal aunt; Shanta, my two fabulous sisters; Nirmisha and Reshma and last but not least, my two incredible children, Nikhil and Kajal, who are my pride and joy. THANK YOU.

This book has been a seed, an idea in the making, for over a decade now. I could not have brought it to life and into fruition without the encouragement and support of my brilliant publisher, Kevin Long of BabySteps Publishing and awesome ghostwriter (who shall remain nameless in line with his wish), who I co-created and wrote this book with. It's been an exciting creative journey. I truly believe that fate brought us all together to share these insights. A huge THANK YOU to you both for your invaluable input and contributions to making this vision and ambition a reality!

I'd also like to acknowledge the artistic genius behind this fabulous book cover, Nisha and my son too, who came up with the mock-up that we opted for in the end. THANK YOU.

I must also acknowledge and appreciate my extended family members, friends, colleagues and coaches who have supported me through various trials and tribulations. Many of you have been my 'knights and knightesses in shining armour' in my hour of need. There are too many of you to list here, but you know who you are, and I am deeply grateful for your support and kindness. THANK YOU.

I can't forget to acknowledge and thank all my clients who have trusted me over the decades in supporting them through their separation and divorce journey. It has been an absolute honour and pleasure to serve each and every one of you through your tough and challenging times. THANK YOU.

Finally, I'd like to acknowledge my ex-spouse, Raj, with who I still remain on good terms, despite our historical challenges and difficulties. Without the colourful life experiences throughout our 31-year relationship; the good, the bad, the ugly, the painful and the joyful, I would not be the person I am today, and we would not have our two amazing children. I am grateful for all these life experiences; they have shaped me, given me deep insights and self-awareness, allowed for personal growth and development and culminated in the creation of this book. THANK YOU.

How To Use This Book

This book isn't meant to be read cover to cover. It's more like a guidebook that you can read in any order and use as a reference book when you get stuck or need some extra guidance. If you like, you can pick and choose chapters that apply to how you're feeling and what you're going through.

It's divided into three parts. The first part, *"Bracing for the Storm"*, focuses on thinking through how to prepare yourself ahead of time to make the divorce process go as smoothly as possible. We'll start by looking at what the divorce situation is like right now in England & Wales and then touch on why a holistic approach to divorce is the way to go. We'll also look at what kind of emotional support you may need to reduce the difficult issues about your marriage and focus on what your life will look like if you try a more proactive approach.

Part two, *"During the Separation - From We to Me"*, helps us transition from the legal side of divorce, where there's a lot of talking, arguing and more talking, to the emotional side, where we can be creative with our co-parenting ideas. We'll find practical ways to use mediation, other dispute resolution options, therapy, coaching and parenting plans and agreements to help you live a better life. You can apply this knowledge in any situation - whether it's being separated, divorced or in limbo between the two - because this book is about how you can create an empowering life for yourself.

The final part, *"After the Divorce - Healing"*, is about creating a new life that brings peace, joy and freedom into your life. It's about creating a healthy relationship with yourself, your children and your ex-spouse. It's about learning to be mindful of what you're feeling so that you can create the life you really want for yourself.

We'll see how you can start over, create new opportunities for yourself, heal old wounds and give you a chance to live your life on your terms. The chapters are arranged so that you can go back to any part of the book and find exactly what you're looking for. Whichever stage you're at in your divorce journey, hopefully, you'll find the guidance that you need to help you get through this difficult transition in your life.

Are you ready to find out about this new way of looking at divorce and separation? Let's do this!

Introduction

Life throws random curve balls at you every once in a while (or, in my case, way too often!) that you can't see coming. The universe loves teaching us lessons in experiences that we may not like. When you think about it, it's rather amusing. Isn't there a better way to teach us lessons? Why can't we have a classroom in the sky with a teacher that just pops out to explain things in a way that will work out best for all the family?

In my case, getting divorced was a painful and transformative experience, like a butterfly coming out of its cocoon. I was compelled to follow the advice and guidance that I had given repeatedly to my divorce and mediation clients over the past decades, to keep everything in perspective, not to be bitter, toxic and twisted and to look at the bigger picture. I had been handed plenty of lemons, and the universe was shouting, "Make lemonade!" I decided that I would not view my divorce as a negative experience. I would use it to learn and grow and to make my life better. We all have a choice in life on how we deal with any given situation and the cards that we are dealt with. Sh*t happens; it's how you deal with it that counts.

I believe that the only way to move past something so destructive as a divorce is to try to be as positive and realistic as possible. What I mean by this is that you need to look at both the good and bad events in your life and not just dwell on the bad parts. The power of being an optimist is that it makes you look at both sides of the coin.

We can't control the events around us, but we can control how we respond to them. Being able to change your perspective of an event from a negative one to a more positive one will not only help you feel better about yourself and your life, but it will also help you move forward in a healthy way. Our mental core has a very direct effect on how we feel about our life in general. Our thoughts can make us happy, or they can make us sad.

Most people are familiar with how the simple act of faking a smile when we're upset can make us feel better, but the same thing applies to our thoughts. When we change our perspective of the situation, we change how we feel about it. Our ability to choose how we see our lives is how we're able to move into a more positive space that helps us create a much better life for ourselves and our children.

We can't change the past, but we can learn from it and move forward in a healthier way than before. This is true not only for major life events like divorce but also in more minor aspects of our lives too. Losing a job, for example, is a very devastating event for many people. But if we choose to live in the past, looking at the things we did wrong and making the same mistakes, we're not going to move forward. We're going to have a lot harder time than creating a better life for ourselves.

Are you ready to live a better life than you're living today? Are you ready to view divorce and divorce lawyers in a more positive light? Are you ready to take control of your own life? If so, let's do this! The best way to move past something difficult is to take on a positive "can do" attitude.

I'm not saying that being positive alone will fix everything, but it's an important first step. When I was going through my own divorce, my biggest strength was seeing the situation more objectively and from my ex-spouse's perspective. As a result, I was not easily upset by circumstances and was able to make a quicker recovery from the trauma of the breakup.

As a person who has experienced a lot of life challenges, I have found ways to remain positive, upbeat and balanced during the toughest of times. "HOLISTIC DIVORCE: Sh*t Happens, It's How You Deal With It That Counts" is a book that is birthed out of my professional and personal experiences to date.

It has given me new insights into things that I would never have thought possible. I'm sharing these perspectives with you in the hope that they'll give you new ways to think about your life and your choices.

Here's to new beginnings and happier, healthier, and more fulfilled lives post-separation and divorce!

PART ONE:

BRACING FOR THE STORM

CHAPTER 1:

A FAMILY SEPARATED WITHOUT BEING DESTROYED

<u>Divorce in the UK, in numbers</u>

In the UK, the divorce rate is estimated to be 42%. This means that out of every ten marriages, on average, four will end in divorce. This is a clear indication that marriages are no longer lasting "until death do us part" and standing the test of time. Those figures are reflected everywhere. We see similar numbers in the United States, and it's worse there, with 50% of first marriages ending in a divorce, 67% of second marriages, where the first failed, and 74% of third marriages.

The only countries with lower divorce rates are in the Far East, where a solid culture of family values is deeply ingrained in their society. Sure, we could say there's a link between culture, family values and the likelihood of a successful marriage, but this isn't a book on how to make a successful marriage; it's about preparing for divorce.

For those of you with a strong belief that divorces are wrong and shouldn't happen, I respect that, but we can't just simply ignore the fact that millions get divorced every year worldwide. The Office of National Statistics confirms that there were 113,505 divorces in the UK in 2021, a 9.6% increase compared to the previous year when there were 103,592 divorces.

"Unreasonable behaviour" was the most common reason cited for divorce under the previous fault-based English divorce laws. We now have the new "no-fault divorce" law in place that came into effect in April 2022. Thankfully, this is taking couples away from the "blame game", and we're starting to see a possibility of a "win-win" situation where both parties are encouraged to focus on an amicable separation where selfishness and blame are left at the door, and a nasty, contentious divorce can be avoided.

What's a holistic approach to divorce?

If I could put a price on divorce and sorting out child arrangements and finances via the litigation and court route for a non-complex case, I'd say that divorcing couples spend, on average, around £20,000 each just in legal costs.

This is a guestimate that I'm sure many lawyers would say is a conservative estimate. This is just the financial costs. We haven't looked at how mentally taxing and emotionally draining the whole process is and the negative effects it has on the parties' relationship with each other, their children, extended family members and friends. When choosing the court route, people tend to only consider the financial costs.

A holistic approach to divorce considers the physical, emotional and mental impact of the process on the parties and their children. It is more likely to feature mediation than the court system. It is also more likely that counselling and therapy will be suggested and recommended to support a healthy transition. Coming from a holistic perspective, we are not just dealing with legal and physical separation but also with a potential breakdown of parenting and support systems for any children impacted by the separation and divorce.

When a relationship ends, and the separated couple have to negotiate their new roles as co-parents, misunderstandings and the healing process between them can take a very long time. Both parties might have to move away from the family home and find places to live separately. It can take a year or more for this transition to take place. During this time, both parents may be forced to co-exist under the same roof while they are transitioning.

Both parties will be going through a lot of upheavals, as well as feeling grief, loss, confusion and even anger. They might feel helpless about whether this process will ever be over and that things can't go back to the way they were.

A holistic approach considers the whole range of emotions during a divorce. It doesn't simply focus on the legal rights and responsibilities of the parties and their children.

A lot of the time, it doesn't feel like a legal process or what other people might perceive as one. By definition, *a holistic process looks at the whole picture to find solutions that will benefit everyone.* It might not be what the court or lawyers will determine as "fair", but it is about finding bespoke resolutions that could benefit everyone involved and solutions that both parties can live with.

The holistic approach to divorce will help parents acknowledge and recognise their feelings and the feelings of their children. This will help them begin the journey of rebuilding a new relationship with each other and their children.

Why a holistic approach to divorce?

The most obvious advantage of a holistic approach to divorce is that it offers a complete solution. It helps and supports parties to address legal rights and responsibilities; it is child-centred and ensures that the children's needs are met first and foremost and allows both parties time to move on with their lives at their own pace.

A holistic approach to divorce has been found to improve relationships between ex-spouses after divorce because each party was able to feel heard and understood. They were able to express their feelings and see what the other was going through; they were more likely to sympathise with one another. They aren't left in resentment because they didn't fully understand what was happening inside of their ex-spouse's head while they were going through tough and challenging times.

These are the benefits:

It is less expensive.

With a holistic approach, couples have the benefit of saving themselves and all involved time, money and energy that they would have spent on a conflict resolution process in the court system. If you have been through the court system, you will be aware of just how much time, money and energy is spent on this process.

It is usually faster.

With a holistic approach to divorce comes an emphasis on finding compromises that both parties can live with and are happy with, reducing conflict. By doing this, the parties can move on faster with their new lives post-completion of their divorce.

Mediators are trained specifically to support both parties in their divorce journey as third-party neutrals. They are there to give the separating couple an opportunity to express their feelings and identify areas of agreement that can be beneficial to everyone involved.

If mediation is used, the need for the court process will be evaluated by the mediator rather than the parties' lawyers. This means that money that may have been spent on legal fees is saved, and more time can be spent looking at "soft topics", such as tools and resources to help parents communicate and co-parent better. These areas are often overlooked by lawyers and would not be considered by a judge, who will usually only focus and adjudicate on legal rights and responsibilities.

You are likely to have more control over your future and co-parenting relationships.

Through mutual support and understanding, it is easier for both parents to rebuild their relationship with each other. The parents then have more control over their future parenting roles and can be open and honest with one another.

We see this happening in our daily lives when separated couples come together, for the greater good of their children, on their own terms. They do not need to depend on court orders that dictate arrangements for their children and all the other legal rights and responsibilities that are secured through the court system.

You will be able to return to a happier, healthier life sooner.

The healing side of a divorce is more likely to happen when you have support from others and those around you. This can be someone who is helping you through the process, whether they are a family member, friend, counsellor or divorce coach.

By having support in the process, rather than just having to cope on your own, it is more likely that your healing and recovery will be quicker. This can also reduce feelings of depression as well as anxiety as you return to living life in a new way.

Children will not feel angry towards their parents.

Parental alienation can happen in a situation where one of the parents is angry with the other, and they do not want the children to have contact with the other parent leading to manipulation of the child's feelings to the extent that they take on the feelings of the angry parent.

One parent may use the children as pawns, trying to get back at their ex-spouse to punish them for leaving. This can sometimes cause the children to fall out of love with one parent and carry feelings of anger that might not be directed towards the parent who is angry.

Parents need to understand that parental conflict is one of the top 10 adverse childhood experiences (ACEs) that children suffer - it is the parental conflict and not the separation and divorce that impacts adversely on children's emotional and psychological well-being.

By introducing a new holistic approach to separation and divorce, where each party can discuss their feelings and emotions with the other, it is more likely that children will maintain a close relationship and bond with both parents and will have a more positive outlook on their future after this process has come to an end.

Where the four states meet

Our *'mental state'* refers to the state of our mind and our ability to think rationally. A clouded mental state means we can't think clearly and logically. This is caused by negativity, anger, hurt and resentment. The divorce process is often accompanied by anxiety, stress and uncertainty, which all take a toll on our thinking. If left unchecked, this can mean we don't have the mental capacity and headspace we need to make good decisions. We may be unable to concentrate fully and not be able to think clearly.

The *'physical state'* refers to our bodies. People go through all sorts of physical and mental changes following divorce, from sleepless nights and poor diet to anxiety, stress and depression. When people feel stressed out about their divorce, they may eat more food, drink more alcohol, take drugs, smoke excessively and avoid exercise leading to an adverse impact on both their physical and mental health.

The *'emotional state'* is the state of how we are feeling. When our emotions are balanced in a healthy way with our thoughts, we can remain calm and make rational decisions. If they aren't balanced, it can lead to anxiety, stress, negative thinking, and an inability to sleep well. When this happens over a long period, we may begin to feel tired and lethargic and lack motivation, leading to decisions that don't serve our family or us.

Our emotional state represents our emotional well-being or lack of it. It is affected by our physical and mental states, which influences us emotionally. While in a positive emotional state, we can think positively, be compassionate towards others and be positive in our outlook on life.

Our *'spiritual state'* is the state connected to our core values, beliefs and purpose or "higher self." This state is often misunderstood or not recognised unless spirituality is within your practice. If we are connected to our higher self, we feel a connection to all, and are open to building good relationships with others and maintaining compassion for others. We can keep an open mind.

When we are spiritual, we can take a step back from what is happening and look at the bigger picture. Being spiritual means, we can use our thoughts and feelings for the greater good of all by inviting peace, happiness and tranquillity into our lives and the lives of others.

When one part (*state*) of our being is affected in a negative way, the rest of our being is affected in a negative way too.

As you can see, the four states are connected, and if one state is off-kilter, this can negatively impact the other states; a holistic approach means we take them all into account. Equally, a healthy state of one or more of the four states can help improve another state that is off balance.

A technique for making permanent life decisions.

The decision to get a divorce is one that, for most people, is overwhelmingly difficult. Even after all the arguments, accusations, and hurt feelings; even after crushing disappointment, loneliness, boredom and disillusionment - divorce still seems like a foreign place that people stare into despondently from a great distance. Most people have built their lives around marriage and family, and it is difficult to let those things go - this is what has defined them.

However, divorce can be a positive life-changing decision if we approach it with the right attitude. Divorce can lead to better relationships with your children; better relationships with your other family members; better relationships with yourself; more fulfilling friendships; more fulfilling professional relationships.

Even if you feel that you are making the right decision to get divorced, it is still going to be a very painful and difficult road to travel. You will have conflicting emotions about your soon-to-be ex-spouse, and you will have anxiety about what the future holds for you.

How can you be sure that you're making the right decision? Here's a way to approach the decision of whether or not to get divorced. This technique of *'visualising'* or rehearsing the outcomes of staying in the marriage or choosing to get a divorce is an excellent way to make an informed decision. I have separated the visualisation into two parts:

First, imagine yourself in 5 years staying married to your spouse. How do you feel? Are you happy? Are you fulfilled and excited about the future? Are you continuing with your life's goals, or have they been side-lined in favour of a marriage where your spouse is unappreciative and unfulfilling?

Next, imagine yourself in 5 years having gotten a divorce. How do you feel about yourself now; how do you feel about your ex-spouse; how will your children be affected by the divorce; how will you handle being alone for the first time (or maybe again)?

Close your eyes and picture yourself with your ex-spouse. Picture what you think the future will hold in 5, 10, and 20 years' time. Compare that to the above visualisation of your life in 5 years if you get a divorce.

When doing this visualisation, do not focus on who is right or wrong, and whose fault it is that you're getting a divorce. Do not focus on what would have happened if you had done things differently - *just focus on being honest about how each outcome makes you feel.* Make up a list of your thoughts about each outcome. Don't worry about being too wordy - just use your best judgement. Sometimes, it's easier to write out things than to say them. (Write them in the format of a question: "If our marriage ends in 5 years, what will I regret?").

Put your ego aside. Be honest with yourself. Be honest about what you're going to miss and what you're ready to leave behind. You might surprise yourself with the answers that you find.

This technique draws answers from our subconscious mind, the part of us that makes decisions without much conscious input. This method can help you make the best decision for you, in the moment and in the future.

Most people feel that a divorce is hugely self-destructive and something that no rational person would do. How can we be honest about it? This technique helps with this dilemma by giving us a different way of looking at things by allowing us to tell ourselves what we need to hear instead of what we think we should say. *It's about tuning into our higher self and intuitive voice* - making more mindful and conscious decisions.

Is the D-Word the right answer?

While there's no general agreement as to when and how a marriage should be ended, there are many signs that will show up in most marriages before a divorce occurs.

When there's abuse and breach of trust

One or both spouses are physically abused, financially abused, emotionally abused, verbally abused - whatever form it takes, it's not acceptable. One or both spouses may feel like they no longer want to stay in their marriage and recognise that they deserve better. One or both spouses may feel undermined, inadequate or worthless in the marriage due to the ill-treatment.

When there's infidelity

In the same way, a husband and wife might be having an affair with someone else - and they're cheating on each other. Either of the spouses may start to feel that their marriage is meaningless, that their spouse is insignificant because he or she is capable of cheating on their spouse. A spouse might find information about the other's affair or catch him or her in the act or in an implicating situation. The other spouse might deny everything, causing more damage to the marriage.

Faithfulness and loyalty are two of the most important elements of any marriage, and when they're broken, it hurts both spouses. The spouse who is cheating will feel guilt and shame, and the spouse who was being cheated upon will begin to feel a lack of self-worth and be angry, hurt by and disappointed with the cheating spouse.

When there's resentment

This is when one or both spouses doesn't feel that they are getting what they need out of the marriage. In some cases, this can mean that one or both spouses are not receiving physical intimacy from their spouse anymore. It can also mean that they're not getting emotional support or that they're not feeling appreciated by their spouse.

When there's no intimacy

Intimacy isn't just about the physical encounters two lovers have. It's about "being in love" with the person you're in a relationship with. Intimacy is about talking, joking and laughing with each other. It's about understanding each other's needs and concerns.

And intimacy is also about sharing your most personal thoughts and feelings with each other. Without that, a marriage becomes shallow and meaningless; just two people who happen to live together in the same household, doing whatever they feel like without really caring what it does to the other spouse.

When there's no longer any respect for each other

Respecting your spouse is about not making fun of him or her in front of someone else. It's about letting your spouse know when you think he or she is wrong in a kind and thoughtful manner.

It's about being humble and admitting when you're in the wrong so that your spouse can respect you for it - even if he or she doesn't agree with what you did. In the same way, it's about giving your spouse the benefit of the doubt, believing the best instead of always thinking that the worst happened, even when it feels better to think differently.

Unity in a marriage is about equal status and rights and having complete trust and faith in one another. Both should feel respected, trusted and appreciated. It's also about accepting that your spouse may make mistakes but trying not to be defensive when he or she makes a mistake.

You'll know that getting a divorce is the right choice for you when you have unmet needs that your spouse cannot address, or your spouse can't get what they need out of the marriage. When you're no longer feeling like you have something to lose, and the hurt and pain are gone. When you're no longer afraid of being alone or losing your children or losing material possessions or taking action that will leave you financially and emotionally insecure. When your self-esteem is back in line with who you really are.

This subject is a lot more complex than I've presented, but hopefully, this gives you some insight.

What "winning" in a separation case looks like

A separation case isn't something to be "won" or "lost." Being granted a court order giving you primary care of your child isn't "winning" a case. What is important is for both parties to come to an amicable agreement that is fair according to the circumstances present at the time, including any dependent children involved.

A divorce may include sorting out arrangements for children, property and finance; it's important for the parties to address these issues in an appropriate and fair manner. If they need to be addressed at all. This is because a separation case isn't actually about the legal issues that arise, but it's more about coming to terms with the fact that the marriage has come to an end, and while the parties have to part, it doesn't have to be an all-out war.

What makes mediation a powerful solution is that it gives both parties the freedom to discuss their issues in a safe, non-judgemental space and with complete privacy.

But before they can do this, they'll have to learn how to talk to each other without getting emotionally involved and triggered, which is an essential part of a successful mediation session. Emotions play a key role in a divorce and separation case, and they often cloud our judgment when it comes to resolving issues, as explained in the above section, 'Where the four states meet'.

PART TWO:

DURING THE SEPARATION - FROM WE TO ME

CHAPTER 2:

ADMITTING THAT IT'S OVER

Emotionally, you are no longer in love with your spouse. You've tried to tell yourself that you're just going through a rough patch, but then you realised that the rough patch has been lasting for years. You may not be able to pinpoint when the love faded, but you know it just isn't there.

You're not sure if you have the strength to go through with a divorce, but you know that's what you need to do. In this chapter, we're going to look at how the challenging transition from 'we to me' occurs and how to stay centred and focused in the face of uncertainty.

<u>The overlapping phases of grief</u>

For me, going through divorce felt like going through what I coined a *"living bereavement"*. It was the death of a long-term, meaningful relationship, my marriage but without a cremation or burial and with no last rights. All the emotions that separation and divorce entail are in tune with death and bereavement. So, to thrive and not just survive after experiencing this grief, we must be kind and compassionate to ourselves, our exes and others impacted by the divorce.

Kubler-Ross, a 1960s psychiatrist who worked with terminal patients, wrote a book that would become a bible for anyone struggling with the loss of a loved one. After observing terminally ill patients and their transitions from living to dying, she concluded that there are five stages of grief. Each person passes through these phases at a different pace and in different ways, but the stages are very similar. The initial model has since been modified and updated a few times, but the idea of stages still stands.

The model consists of five stages: denial, anger, bargaining, depression and acceptance. The stages are not necessarily linear, and you can go back and forth from one stage to another. *Denial* is when you don't accept reality, and you try to pretend that nothing has changed. When you're going through denial, it's very easy to think that things will get better or turn around overnight. This can make us feel hopeful for a short period of time before we realise that hope is misplaced, and the pain continues to accumulate in our hearts.

In the case of a rocky marriage, denial is when you believe that you're in a rough patch and that it will pass. *Anger* and frustration come next when we realise that things aren't getting better, and we start to feel annoyed and angry at our spouses.

Bargaining is when we try to negotiate with our spouse to come back to us because we can't accept that they've left us. In this stage, we'll do whatever it takes to make them come back to us and be willing to compromise as much as possible in order for them to stay. In the event of a cheating spouse, this stage can last a very long time after the infidelity has been committed.

In the *depression* stage, we may become angry, but we no longer have the energy to fight or make a scene. We're too tired and unmotivated to be anything other than sad and disappointed in ourselves. Even if we try to complain, nobody will listen to us because their focus is elsewhere. We don't want people to feel sorry for us, so we keep our feelings bottled up inside of us until they explode like a volcano and erupt when it all gets too much for us.

Acceptance comes when we can no longer deny the truth: that the marriage isn't salvageable and, in our opinion, should be over. We no longer keep hope alive that "we'll make it" or that "things will get better."

Acceptance is very different from giving up, and it's also a lot more powerful than the other four stages combined. This is the moving forward phase, where we start to take action and make plans for the future. In this stage, we start looking into all the possibilities that lie ahead of us and, in most cases, we don't want to go back to our old way of life.

When it comes to marriage in transition, the grief stages often overlap as one moves into another. This can make it extremely difficult to determine what stage you're really in since they all affect one another. For example, bargaining can quickly turn into denial when we realise that our partner isn't coming back to us, which can lead to anger as our spouse continues to walk out the door.

Finding peace in the storm

There will be a lot of stress during the separation process, and it's important to remember that everyone has a different response and threshold to stress. Some people handle it better than others, and there are some things that can increase someone's anxiety levels.

This can range from something as simple as not sleeping well to more intense things like yelling and screaming at your spouse in front of guests or friends. In this section, we'll be sharing some ways to keep things in perspective and to reduce the overall stress of the separation process.

When taking a break to go outside and to get some fresh air won't work, try some of these ways to get your mind off of things and to concentrate on the present moment. Most people can get a lot more done when they're calm and relaxed.

It starts with learning the process beforehand. By reading this book, you've already made the first step towards taking control of the separation process for you and for your spouse. This is the most important thing that you'll do during this event, and you may find that it's the biggest hurdle to overcome. Once you've realised that there's a problem, it can feel like there's nothing else to do but react and panic. But by educating yourself, you're empowering yourself to take steps toward positive change.

Getting some perspective on things by looking at what causes crises during a separation is an important step in being proactive instead of reactive. By being on the lookout for potential problems, you're much less likely to become overwhelmed by them. Instead of panicking when you start to feel a crushing sense of fear and frustration, try these simple steps to get your mind off of it. Then, accept that this too shall pass.

Revisit that time in the past when you were anxious. It could have been before a job interview for that position you desired, a big speech, or even a big date. Think back on times in the past when anxiety was present and how it affected you. Do you remember how it didn't turn out as bad as you had expected?

Our minds love catastrophising, which refers to imagining the worst possible outcomes. This can make us feel scared and worried about the future, but it's important to realise that fear and panic can often prevent true problems from occurring. When something happens, we want to be prepared for it without panicking or feeling unprepared, right? In this case, try looking at your relationship with stress and anxiety.

Look at things in perspective by taking a deep look at what's going on in your life. Before you know it, these things will be a distant memory, and you'll be able to view them with a more positive outlook. Take small, consistent steps towards change by making adjustments that are manageable. Small and simple changes can have a huge positive impact on your attitude and mood. This includes things like starting to meditate and practicing breathing techniques, as we'll see in part three of this book, *After the Divorce - Healing.*

Consider talking to a divorce counsellor or coach. Find a counsellor or coach who is open-minded about the things you may be going through and is willing to listen without judging or preaching about their own agenda. The goal isn't to keep your marriage together but rather to help you through the separation process.

A neutral third party can be a great sounding board for you as you go through the separation process. Talking to them will help you to relax and realise that you're not alone in this, that others have gone through it, and that they've survived. Friends and family can be a great source of support during the separation process, but you may find that you're experiencing cognitive dissonance. This is when you know that the person wants to support you, but at the same time, you're still in denial about the problems in your marriage.

Please don't judge yourself for feeling this way. It's natural for family and friends to propose that you reconcile, but they may not have been married long themselves and are not in your shoes. Your mind can trick you into thinking that this is a "fairy tale" life where everything works out perfectly.

But do try to view your marriage from their perspective and see how it could be worth saving at this point.

Writing down your thoughts, ideas, and feelings can help you to get them out of your head and onto the page. You'll start to see patterns emerge as you write things down, which can often lead to unexpected insights. If nothing else, writing down your thoughts can relieve stress by getting thoughts out of your head and onto the page.

'Journaling' is a way of gaining insight into your thoughts and feelings. It's a form of self-therapy that can help you see what you're feeling, why you're feeling it, and how it will impact your ability to function well in the aftermath.

A notebook can be a great place to start. It's portable and can easily fit in your briefcase or handbag. Writing on paper instead of on a computer screen will help you to concentrate on what you're writing, and it can be easier to express yourself if you don't have the option of editing what you've written. By writing down your thoughts and feelings, you'll understand why you're feeling the way you are.

It may be difficult for some people to express themselves in words. If this is the case, just write it as if you were talking into a tape recorder. Don't worry about punctuation, spelling or grammar. Just get your ideas and thoughts out on paper.

Making notes on postcards is a fun way to make writing more enjoyable and to get creative to help you express yourself. Making rough sketches of ideas and concepts is another great way to express yourself. It's also a good way to get a visual representation of your thoughts and feelings. Drawing can be therapeutic and can help you to visualise things that can be difficult to express in words.

A healthy outlet for emotions

Wouldn't it be great if the human brain had a reset button that could reset our emotional state? In the same way that we reset our routers when the Wi-Fi is acting up or when we restart our phones, if they are malfunctioning, we should be able to reset our emotions to a happier state.

We do have a reset button, but it's not as simple as clicking a remote control. It takes more work than that; we need to be patient. You can't really change the circumstances of your life, but you can change the way you respond. It takes time, energy, patience and creativity to make a better life.

Before we look at a few suggested healthy ways of dealing with your emotions, I want you to answer this question.

What do you do when you need to "blow off steam?" Let's say that you've had a bad day or a particularly hard week. What do you do when you need to get away from it all?

Do you vent to your spouse? Do you vent to someone else? Do you go for a run or take a drive? Do you go and have a drink with friends? Do you binge-watch Netflix until the early hours of the morning or avoid going to bed all night to avoid dealing with your emotional state? Whatever actions you take, they are all forms of venting. Venting is a healthy emotional outlet in the beginning, but if you continue to vent in unhealthy ways, it becomes self-destructive to your emotional state.

These are a few ways you can vent your emotions during these tough and challenging times.

Let's start with something we all love:

Take part in your hobby

Hobbies are a great way to deal with stress. It means doing something you enjoy, which takes your mind off the situation at hand. Pick something you've wanted to do for a while now but just haven't had time to do. Pick something that makes you happy and brings you joy. Taking the weekend off to visit your favourite adventure park, trying out that sport you always wanted to play or taking up dance classes. I took up salsa classes several months after my separation to lift my spirits, as dancing brings me joy.

If you're the creative type, do something related to your passion. Write like you have no idea what you'll say next; try painting with watercolours or even just sketching. Do what lights you up, and don't let anything hold you back!

If you don't have a hobby, then it's time to look for one. Hobbies that challenge our creativity, like making jewellery, making origami or installing fairy lights, are a great way to let off some steam. If you like being outdoors, then a hobby like hiking, star gazing or going for long walks in the park can be very therapeutic.

Starting a hobby after a divorce may sound odd, but trust me, it feels good. It programs your brain that you have time to take care of yourself and that you still have things to look forward to. It feels good knowing that you can still do the things that make you happy; in fact, it feels great!

Working on your hobby will save you from wasting time watching reruns of *Friends* or *The Office* for the umpteenth time!

Trace your family tree

A seemingly unrelated activity like this can help you connect with your past and future. It's very therapeutic in the sense that it lets you know that although your situation may be difficult right now, you can still appreciate everything good going on in your life. You can look back and appreciate all the people who have been there for you and who are still there for you. It's a way of saying thanks for all the good times, and it gives a taste of what's to come in life.

Even if it ends up being a wild goose chase, at the very least, you will have diverted your attention from your troubles for a short time.

Read something inspiring

Reading about divorce or the struggles of others can help you realise that you are not the only one going through this. Try reading stories from other people going through similar situations, and it may even help keep you grounded in reality.

It helps you to realise that although things may look bad right now, they could always be worse, and although things may seem hopeless right now, there is always hope. It will really help if the author of the book has been through your situation before and has found a way of dealing with it in a positive manner.

When you read books from authors who have faced divorce, you'll know that whatever situation you're in, it will eventually pass, and it will help sustain your hope and faith when it's running low.

<u>Understanding your role as a spouse and as a parent</u>

Before the divorce, you held two hats: a spouse and a parent. After the divorce, you'll be switching your parent hat for a co-parent one. Making this transition is not an easy one. It's natural for us to feel angry and bitter towards the other party and to feel like the children are suffering because of it. It's not your fault; it's not your ex-spouse's fault, either. Playing "the blame game" at this stage will only be detrimental to your emotional and psychological well-being and won't serve you or the children.

Before, your spouse's role and parent's role were intertwined. Now, they have been separated into two different roles. You may have to occupy multiple roles in the future depending on your situation, but right now, you'll be focusing on your responsibilities as a co-parent.

When you can separate these two roles in your own head, it helps you take a more rational view of things and deal with them accordingly. It also helps you be more patient with the children because they are probably feeling the same emotions that you are feeling. Some may feel sad and rejected, while others may feel confused and angry at the new situation they've found themselves in.

<u>Fighting the temptation to get back with your ex</u>

One of the most difficult situations faced by divorced people is to avoid being in contact with their ex-spouse. Usually, the temptation for contact is so strong that it makes some people return to the life they swore: "never again." Although the phenomenon of returning to a former partner after a divorce is quite common, there are ways to prevent this from happening.

It starts with dismissing the thoughts of ever going back to your ex-spouse

Stop thinking about how much you miss your ex-spouse and reminiscing about the relationship that you used to have. For many people, the feeling of simply being away from the person they used to love causes a deep feeling of sadness. This sadness usually ends up forcing people to make phone calls or send messages to their ex-spouses.

Fill the vacuum

After separation/divorce, the feeling of wanting to get back to your ex may be brought by two things. First, you're looking for someone to vent out to because you're sad.

Who is the first person people in relationships talk to when they're feeling down? It's usually their partner. Now, you're separated/divorced; you don't have a partner to vent to. Secondly, you may be missing the romantic part of the relationship, but this will lead you back to your ex. To avoid these feelings, I recommend you fill that emotional void with friends, family and new activities.

The emotional vacuum can also be filled by a new relationship, but the first thing is to make sure that you're not just looking for a rebound. A rebound relationship can end up more detrimental than beneficial and might even make the breakup last longer than it should. As we shall see in chapter 17, Moving on to new relationships, jumping into casual relationships too quickly can often lead to more problems.

Reflect on why it ended

Anytime you're tempted to call or write a message to your ex, it's a good time to reflect on why the relationship failed. Remind yourself of the circumstances that led you to divorce. This will help you rationalise why you don't want to go back to your ex-spouse.

In this chapter, we've seen that the transition from a married life to a divorced one can cause some stress and confusion in people. It can be quite overwhelming, and it's important to try your best to find some solace in these situations. Being as proactive as possible will help you focus on the positive aspects of divorce rather than the negative ones.

You'll learn to see that you've made the best decision for you and/or you've gotten out of a toxic relationship that wasn't aligned with your core values and goals in life.

Further, you'll learn to see that the outcome of a divorce is not as bad as it may seem at first, and the most important lesson you'll learn is to never give up hope. Divorce and sh*t happens; it's not the end of the world. It's the beginning of a new chapter in your life. What you choose to do with this new chapter will define who you become in the future.

In the next chapter, we'll be looking at how we can deal with the stress that divorce can cause us. Once we understand what causes this stress, we'll be able to deal with it rationally. This will also help you see that you're not alone in feeling the way you do, and you'll realise that these feelings aren't abnormal and that most people around you have gone through it before.

At this point in life, where a clouded mind could push you away from the truth and send you down the wrong path, it's important to have a clear headspace and to know that your mind is capable of taking care of you. You'll learn how to train your mind and how it can be a great tool in your journey of self-discovery.

CHAPTER 3:

DEALING WITH STRESS AND ANXIETY

The palms get sweaty, the heart rate increases, and the mind gets foggy. Haven't I just described an all-too-familiar feeling? It's what happens to us when we're about to go on a date with the man or woman of our dreams. We get the same feeling before a job interview or giving a public speech.

It's that annoying feeling of nerves when you think that you can't do something, but you have to do it anyway. It's what happens when we're asked to give an impromptu speech at a social event. We get nervous, a bit hesitant, and make some mistakes, and our mind starts wondering why we were put in this situation in the first place. It's a feeling that tells us that we're not good enough to do a required task, but it's also a feeling of anticipation because we may be just about to discover something new about ourselves.

Anxiety is the name of this feeling, and it's not just a feeling. It's a condition that can be diagnosed. It's a state of mind characterised by excessive fear, apprehension and tension. In the clinical field of psychology, one can identify specific types of anxiety linked to different types of triggers.

We all experience anxiety sometimes, but what makes it a clinical condition is when it doesn't fade away and becomes unmanageable. This is what happens in the case of *'divorce stress syndrome'*. It's the excessive amount of worry, fear, apprehensiveness and tension that we experience when going through a divorce. It can be very debilitating because it makes us view life through the lens of despair instead of with a positive mindset that keeps us moving forward.

What is Divorce Stress Syndrome (DSS)?

By definition, DSS is a syndrome embodied by the intense emotional and psychological effects on individuals who are involved in a divorce. It is primarily a syndrome precipitated by the sheer stress of the divorce, but it can also be caused by other factors such as work-related issues and financial difficulties.

What does Divorce Stress Syndrome feel like?

DSS is usually characterised by feelings of melancholy over our situation. We keep on reminiscing about what used to be and how wonderful our relationship was. The more we try to move past it, the more we keep thinking about it.

This makes us a victim of our own thoughts and causes us to be stuck in the past. We get stuck because we feel that our past relationship is something that will never exist again, and this causes us to feel sad. It's a feeling where we want to go back, but we know it's impossible or not the right answer.

DSS is also characterised by feelings of guilt, shame, resentment and constant worry about how you're going to deal with your future without your ex-spouse. These feelings stop you from living in the present moment and make you stuck on things that may never happen. This kind of stress leads directly to depression since it deprives you of being active in your recovery process.

How stress and anxiety manifest in our body and mind

Stress and anxiety are two overlapping feelings that are caused by an event that is challenging to us, such as divorce. They both have similar symptoms and can make you feel very uneasy and on edge.

Stress causes our bodies to become more alert and produce more adrenaline, cortisol and other hormones that prepare us to deal with potential threats. In the case of anxiety, one has a sense of being threatened by something unknown or something one can't control.

This sense of being threatened triggers the brain into an alert mode, ready for anything. Typically, we have three stress responses - fight, freeze or flight.

These mental health conditions have adverse manifestations in our day-to-day lives as well.

Let's look at a few of them:

You're Always Worried

You can't focus on anything other than the task at hand, and that feeling of urgency never goes away. You feel extremely tired, irritable, and tense all the time. The brain races and won't stop churning out the same thoughts. To be fair, there's a lot to worry about during the divorce. There is uncertainty about child arrangements, what happens to the family home, assets to be divided, a new home to be found, and finances to be managed.

All these things will cause a lot of stress. What most people fail to realise is that taking this stress into bed with them can lead to insomnia and restless sleep. All night long, you toss and turn, and it takes you hours to get a few hours of sleep if you can get any at all. Having deep sleep and rest should be our number one priority at these times to help us function better.

The sense of urgency won't go away; it only gets worse as time passes by. You have what some call "panic attacks" where your heart races out of control, you feel like you're out of breath, and your body becomes flooded with adrenaline, cortisol and other hormones that prepare us to deal with potential threats.

Crying and bursts of anger

You are also feeling irritable and tense all the time. One of your friends will say they never see you smile anymore. When they ask the reason, you burst into tears and tell them how miserable you feel. There's no reason to cry over the divorce, right? Well, when a divorce is this stressful, any small thing can set you off. It is good to feel and release your emotions and not keep them bottled up, as this can lead to more health issues down the line. The body always keeps a score of our emotions, and this can manifest in other ailments if not released.

A change in appetite

Stress changes our eating habits in either way. We may become binge eaters who seek comfort foods like chocolate, ice cream, pizza, and chips. After eating these foods, we experience a short-term burst of relief and then go back to being depressed. Or, we can lose our appetite and start to forget about meals altogether.

When we were with our spouse, we had a routine that included specific times for eating and maybe having a glass of wine during date night to help us relax. Having dinner together was a big part of our day and a great way to reconnect. Now we're alone, eating alone, and it's not fun. This is what can lead to binge eating or skipping meals entirely when you go through a divorce.

Making good decisions when we're stressed

High-pressure situations are all around us. In the corporate world, managers have to make important business decisions that may impact the company's bottom line. For people in relationships, there are times when we've had a long day, and our spouses expect us to be jovial and cheerful.

During the divorce process, it's hard to have patience with the process and its standards. There's a lot of paperwork that needs to be filled out, court appearances and conferences that take place, so how are you supposed to take it easy? It's all about managing your feelings and focusing on the present.

Be logical, and don't overreact. If you can think through your responses before you say them, then you will be better able to handle whatever comes your way. The simple act of breathing in, does more than you realise. It allows oxygen to enter the body and provides space for more air to be absorbed by your body. Breathing out allows for toxins, carbon dioxide, and other gases to travel out of your body.

Whenever you feel stressed, take three deep breaths, exhaling completely each time. This works as a great tool for taking a mental break from whatever is bothering you. Even if it's just for 5 minutes, deep breathing allows you to relax and reset your mind.

When you're in the middle of a situation that makes you upset and angry, try to hold those feelings back long enough to think about what's really going on underneath and bothering you.

Another technique that works wonders when making decisions is to visualise how things will turn out to be in the next two years if you choose one option. Let's say that you're not sure whether you should initiate the separation or persevere a little longer, hoping things will improve. If you choose the first option, where do you see yourself and your partner two years from now? Do you see both of you living together, struggling to keep things together, and you not being happy at all, or do you envision yourselves living in peace, contentedness and harmony?

A final tip for making decisions when you're stressed is to ask for help and advice. Friends, family members, co-workers or even online networks for those facing similar situations know what you're going through and should be able to guide you. While you'll be the one making the final informed and mindful decision, their input on the matter can make all the difference.

Managing triggers

Transitioning through a divorce isn't easy. The emotions that we'll travel through will include anger, pain, stress, fear, anxiety, depression, loneliness and sadness.

These feelings may come in waves or even hit us like a ton of bricks when we are least expecting them. The best way to combat these feelings is to manage them by identifying their triggers.

A trigger refers to an event, moment, or situation that makes you feel a certain way. For example, if your friends get engaged after you're separated from your spouse, this will be a prime opportunity for you to get upset and start thinking about the things that you're missing out on.

If a divorce is due to infidelity, then there's a chance that we'll be triggered by intimacy signals from other people. We might see a couple holding hands or even kissing, and it can remind us of times when we felt that way with our spouse, only to eventually feel betrayed or wronged.

One way to handle this trigger is to avoid setting ourselves up for failure by mentally preparing for certain events ahead of time. Or, as I did in the first few years after my separation, make a conscious choice not to go to weddings and big family gatherings and withdraw from anything that you know will make you feel bad.

Before you go shopping, acknowledge that you're going to see happy couples with their arms around each other. Having an awareness of when you're likely to be triggered can help you distance yourself from the situation before it happens.

Another way of dealing with this trigger is to ask yourself, "Is it worth being upset?" You'll want to ask this question because if the answer is no, then making yourself feel bad isn't going to help anyone.

People will also ask about how you're handling the divorce and if you're getting along with your ex-spouse. When they ask you if you're doing okay, don't go off on a tangent and start complaining about how difficult this whole ordeal has been.

Be tactful when explaining the reasons why you and your ex are divorcing. If they really want to know more, then give them a brief synopsis of what happened and how it's affected your life. The last thing that you want to do is alienate yourself from the people that care about you.

When you feel that they're crossing the line, you always have the option of politely ending the conversation. Say something like, "It's good that you're asking, but this is a touchy subject, and I'd rather not talk about it right now." It's good to maintain healthy boundaries for your own sanity and peace of mind.

Understand that your friends and family members want to be there for you during this difficult time. They will have a hard time comprehending why you two were not able to work things out, but the best response to this is to listen, validate their concern and let them know that it is appreciated.

Pictures of our ex-spouses or of our former married life will trigger feelings of sadness, regret, anger and resentment. Don't be afraid to remove these things from your life, especially if it's causing you to become upset.

Your social media feeds can also contain items that might be triggering. If you find certain posts or photos upsetting, block them so they will not show up in your feed again. By removing some of the pictures and posts from your social media pages, you'll reduce the chance of being triggered by what you see online. For me personally, coming off Facebook and deleting my account was one of the best decisions I made on the road to my recovery and healing. When going through sh*tty times, the last thing I wanted to view constantly on social media was other people's filtered, perfect lives.

Your children will be a trigger if they ask you about your separation or if they seem upset. When they say they miss their dad or mum, be careful of what you say as it could influence them and have an adverse impact on their emotional and psychological well-being.

The way that children handle these situations will greatly differ from one child to the other, but the same best practices apply. Remember that they are impressionable, and if you're not there to help them cope with the situation, they'll probably end up resenting you.

Remember that your feelings are only temporary, and it's important to limit the time that you spend reflecting on past events or dwelling on the future. If possible, try to avoid stressful situations or people who will trigger your emotions as much as possible.

Emotional meltdowns

An emotional meltdown refers to a situation where you feel as though you are being overwhelmed, unable to cope and where a certain event may cause you to lose control. There are many things that could trigger an emotional meltdown, such as a simple disagreement with someone, your children being upset about going to school or being overwhelmed by the fact that you have to take care of the house and children on your own.

There are many ways of dealing with an emotional meltdown, and most of these have to do with your outlook on life. Try not to dwell on the negatives and instead focus on the good. If you have problems going about this on your own, you may want to seek out professional help or talk to someone who knows what you're going through.

If possible, try out different coping mechanisms until you find one that works for you.

These are three techniques that may help you:

Waiting it out

Instead of using confrontation as your primary strategy, try being more passive by overlooking the problem. This method of dealing with an emotional meltdown will require you to resist any urges to talk it out or address the problem head-on.

Resist the urge to go on social media or have discussions with people about what's bothering you. Instead, practice patience to keep yourself from getting upset.

Not dealing with your emotions doesn't mean that you're ignoring them; you're exercising self-restraint at a time when you'd otherwise be prone to act impulsively and say things you don't mean and may later regret.

When we don't react to the situation, our thoughts and feelings have time to simmer down, giving us time to think of the best way to respond and handle things later on.

Distract yourself

If you feel like you're going to have an emotional meltdown, it could be caused by stress or simply because your thoughts are running wild, and you don't know how else to stop them.

The best way of handling this is to distract yourself either through calming activities, or taking a break from the situation for a few minutes. By temporarily removing yourself from your present situation, you give yourself a chance to reflect on it and check in to see if this is really something worth stressing about.

Physical activity is one of the best ways of dealing with stress, as it allows you to take a mental break amidst all the chaos. If you are having a hard time coping, try breathing techniques or exercise and use this to calm your nervous system. The simple act of just taking a 5-10 minute walk with deep breathing can be a very powerful exercise to calm your nervous system.

When you are feeling overwhelmed or stressed, it's tempting to want to shut down your feelings and put on a brave face. You may want to act like everything is fine, even when you'd rather cry than smile. By acting this way, you're not serving your needs.

Be easy on yourself

Be kind to yourself. Stop blaming yourself for things that you can't control, and don't beat yourself up for the things that you cannot change. It's okay to feel sad, guilty and angry, but it's not right to keep this bottled up inside of you.

Instead of cursing those who caused you pain, it would be better if you were able to forgive them and yourself. Forgiveness allows us to move on in our lives and soothes our feelings by releasing tension gradually.

Remember that forgiveness is not something that's easy to do, but it is something that we should work towards because every time we hold onto anger or resentment towards someone else, we are allowing ourselves to be held hostage to the past events and staying stuck, which causes us even more pain.

Staying in the past will not help you move on with your life, and it will not help you get over your emotional pain. Forgiveness will give you the peace of mind that you need to move on with your life. If we do not forgive those who have done us wrong, we cannot hope to be forgiven for our own shortcomings. We're all human, and none of us are perfect - we all make mistakes.

Where's this anger coming from?

When anger spirals out of control, there's no denying that it can make you feel helpless and even hopeless. Getting angry at the people in your life could be a way to vent your frustration towards something that you can directly blame for the breakdown of your relationship, but it could also cause more harm than good.

Although it's natural to feel angry when going through a divorce, this anger can be detrimental to your emotional health. As a result, it's important to be wary of the negative consequences that could arise from acting out in such a rageful manner.

When you are feeling the urge to lash out at other people, take a deep breath and try to slow down your thoughts before jumping into action. When you're in the midst of a divorce, it's hard to control your impulse or self-control, but as time passes by, you will start to see things more clearly, and with a clearer mind, you will have a better understanding of what's going on.

Resist the urge and temptation to seek revenge on your ex-spouse and, instead, find different ways of dealing with the negative feelings that could make you angry. Don't blame others or take out your frustrations on other family members or even friends since this won't benefit your own well-being and it only adds more pressure to your life.

It's crucial to keep an eye on what's important and what isn't. For instance, if you experience a fit of rage after finding out that your ex had an affair, try to think of what really matters in your life right now.

Instead of taking out your frustration on other people, talk to a counsellor or psychotherapist about how you can put your painful emotions aside for now. If you feel that this anger is affecting your daily life and making it hard for you to function normally, then anger management classes might be beneficial to help you better understand and deal with your emotions.

Cultivating positive emotions, forgiving others (and ourselves), healing and not being angry is the best way of dealing with your rage; this is an important step that we should all take towards moving forward instead of staying stuck in the past.

Visualising cutting the marital bond

In a previous section on making decisions when we're under pressure, we saw that we could make better decisions by imagining how different our life would be in the future if we chose a certain option. By doing that, we were visualising the good things that would come from the decision and not being swayed by the outcome or other factors.

The practice of imagining what we want our future to look like is known as *'visualisation.'* You can visualise almost anything you want. Imagine, for example, the relationship you want to have with your children, the house you want to live in or the career you want. Visualising is a tool for bringing about change. It helps us to set goals, improves self-awareness, helps us understand how to attain something and, as a result, makes it more likely that what we envision will come true. Taking action towards making your vision a reality is the key; visualisation alone will not bring about tangible change.

Visualising allows us to create our new reality by setting goals and knowing what we really want in life. So how do we use this method of psychological change when healing after a divorce? *The law of attraction* says that we attract into our lives whatever we're thinking about, so be mindful of where you place your attention.

By visualising a happy, single life as a result of your divorce, you are creating a positive outlook for your future. This doesn't mean that your divorce will be without pain or that you're meant to be single. It simply means that by visualising the future you want - whether it's single or married - you are more likely to create experiences and opportunities for those things to materialise in your life.

Visualise yourself happy, healthy and having a great life - this is the key to letting go of anger and embracing happiness. Let go of any grudges or bitterness towards others who have let you down in life and set yourself free from the past.

To do this, go to a quiet place. A bedroom is a good place or even a park bench on a beautiful day. Close your eyes and picture yourself signing your divorce papers to confirm that you will no longer be married to your ex-spouse. Think of the advantages that this divorce brings about. Think of all the negatives, too.

Realise that no matter how hard the divorce has been for you, it's one of the best things that could have happened. Your spouse is gone, and you no longer have to deal with their issues, their problems and their bad habits. Try to think about exactly what you're going through during your divorce - write it down on a piece of paper and read it out loud. This helps us acknowledge our problems but also helps us feel free from them too by writing them out and having an outlet.

How we think and how we feel about what's going on in our life can affect our emotional well-being. We've also seen that the way we respond to our emotions is something that's within our control - even if we don't feel currently capable of controlling our emotions.

We have also explored some of the ways in which our emotions can affect us throughout and after divorce, as well as some ways in which they could make us happier. We've seen that through learning techniques and skills, there are ways that we can change even small negative experiences into positive ones and shift our energy, vibrations and frequency from low to high.

In the next chapter, we're going to see how mediators can help us come to amicable resolutions about issues arising out of your separation and divorce. Instead of going down the court route and being stuck in a drawn-out court battle, mediation will help you settle matters quickly and economically.

CHAPTER 4:

MEDIATION

At a basic and simplistic level, there are three ways to end a marriage and sort out issues:

1) Battling it out in court, where both sides plead their case with or without the support of lawyers – where a judge or bench of magistrates determine outcomes.
2) Having a mediator help you settle out of court and then take legal advice to formalise agreements reached.
3) Doing it yourself where you'll come to mutual agreements with your spouse and then take legal advice to formalise agreements reached.

Each of these methods of ending a marriage has various advantages and disadvantages.

What if circumstances in your marriage make it difficult for you both to agree on how to share the assets or sort out child arrangements? These problems can be addressed by having a third-party neutral mediator engaged in providing legal and other information, guidance, tools, resources and possible solutions that could help you move forward with your lives after your divorce.

In this chapter, we'll see exactly how mediation helps both parties and what benefits it offers them above going to court or handling everything on their own.

What is family mediation?

Family Mediation is an out-of-court dispute resolution option facilitated by the mediator who acts as a third-party neutral. The mediator helps participants to:

1) Communicate better.
2) Be future-focused.
3) Make their own informed decisions about some or all the issues relating to their separation, divorce, children, property, finances and other non-legal issues like agreeing to boundaries and on how to best communicate with one another.

Mediation gives both sides the opportunity to have their say and have their interests represented in any final agreement. It usually works best if the parties have taken some legal advice to manage realistic expectations of their rights and responsibilities.

There are different models of mediation as follows:

The *'traditional model'* is where a sole mediator hosts mediation with both parties in the same room or virtual platform together. Sometimes, in more complex cases, it may be wise to have a co-mediator working alongside the parties.

A variation on the traditional model is *'shuttle mediation'*, which is used to facilitate mediation in cases where the parties cannot share space. In this model, the mediator will go back and forth between the parties who are in separate rooms.

Where there are child arrangement issues, there is the option to consider *'child inclusive mediation'* for children who are of a suitable age, usually 10 years and above. If both parties consent and there is agreement from the children, their voice; wishes and feelings can be ascertained (in a child-appropriate manner by a trained and qualified child-inclusive mediator) to be shared with the parents subject to the child's consent to share information with their parents.

If a case is highly complex or where there are multiple participants, *'hybrid mediation'* may be considered. This is a relatively new concept in England & Wales, where the parties agree to mediate with the support of their lawyers (and other experts that may be needed to advise and assist the parties as third-party neutrals) within the mediation forum.

Mediated agreements are not legally binding in the UK but can be converted into legally binding agreements or court orders. Usually, parties will seek the help of lawyers to finalise these agreements in a legally binding way.

Any terms agreed in mediation can be written up into a *'without prejudice'* summary or memorandum of understanding. A without prejudice document is protected and cannot be used in litigation without both parties' consent to convert into a legally binding agreement or court order by consent.

Normally, for child arrangement agreements, the parties will draw up a *'parenting plan'* to formalise and set out the arrangements agreed upon. A parenting plan represents a working document that can be reviewed at regular intervals to ensure that the arrangements continue to meet the children's best interests and are in line with their wishes and feelings.

Most couples who choose to mediate will be able to resolve their issues in a matter of weeks or months, whereas going to court could take several months and, in many cases, up to 18 months, sometimes longer to conclude.

Since the pandemic, the family courts have had huge backlogs and delays, with cases taking an average of 12 months to conclude. There are increasing complaints from those who work within the sector about many hearings being pulled out of the court diary at short notice due to a shortage of full-time judges.

It's fair to say that the UK family court system is currently on its knees and that these delays are causing those facing family break up greater stress, anxiety and uncertainty.

In April 2021, the government announced that it would be offering vouchers of up to £500 per family to help pay for family mediation. This was seen as a positive move, as it aimed to make the process of mediation more affordable for families who may be struggling with the financial costs of separation or divorce.

The scheme has proven to be successful with research and feedback from participants confirming that around 70% of all mediated cases under the scheme have reached a partial or full agreement. The scheme has been extended to April 2025.

What family mediation isn't

The mediator won't be the one making the decisions. A mediator is not a judge or an arbitrator. Nor are they counsellors or therapists. The role of the mediator is to hold a safe and supported space to facilitate communication between both sides so that they can come to an agreement themselves without interference from anyone else. The mediator isn't there to tell you what to do or how to act, but they will give you relevant information and guidance. Mediators help the parties come up with mutually agreeable resolutions.

The four core principles of mediation

Mediation is a voluntary process

This means that both you and your spouse must agree to mediate. Neither of you can be forced to mediate. It is also voluntary for the mediator, who can withdraw from the process at any stage if the mediation becomes counterproductive or toxic.

In the UK, there is no legal obligation in family law matters to participate in mediation. However, anyone wishing to start court proceedings is expected to attend a Mediation Information and Assessment Meeting (known as a MIAM).

This is an initial individual meeting for the mediator to give information about mediation and other dispute resolution options as well as other helpful information, tools, and resources that are bespoke to your circumstances like, signposting to counselling or coaching services. The other key feature of a MIAM is for the mediator to assess if the matter is *'safe and suitable'* for joint mediation. If one party refuses to attend a MIAM, it is assumed that they don't wish to consider dispute resolution options before going to court to sort out issues.

Mediation is a confidential and legally privileged process

Once you start the mediation process, there is a lot of confidentiality and privilege in place with a few caveats to secure the safety of any vulnerable adults and children and if the mediator is alerted to one or both parties' intention to commit an unlawful act or crime.

This means that none of the contents of your discussions in mediation can be revealed outside of the mediation forum unless for the purposes of taking legal or financial advice in support of the mediation process, strictly on a without prejudice basis. Neither can it be referred to in any future litigation proceedings. This includes any written communication from the mediator.

The decision-making rests with the parties

The mediator will facilitate constructive and pragmatic conversations between you and your ex-spouse to help you both reach your own informed agreements and decisions. The mediator will not determine the outcome for you if you reach an impasse and cannot agree on all or some of the issues.

The mediator is neutral

The mediator will act in an even-handed manner between you and your ex-spouse to help you both reach an outcome that works for you both and your children.

Mediators will encourage parents to be child-centred and focused at all times when exploring issues to consider the impact on them regarding any solutions and agreed outcomes.

This means that neither of you can get the upper hand in the mediation session. The mediator will not side with one party over another.

<u>What mediators do and how they help</u>

Mediators help parties to talk through their issues and have difficult conversations in a safe, confidential and supported environment.

These are the key functions of a mediator:

The mediator opens a channel of communication

A mediator promotes open and transparent discussion between both parties. They are there to help put you at ease and to encourage you to talk without feeling judged or criticised. They help define and clarify areas of disagreement and identify areas of agreement to find common ground.

The mediator challenges unrealistic ideas

In many cases, one of the parties may have set a clear expectation of what they want from the divorce. This expectation could be unrealistic due to their hopes not aligning with the law and their respective legal rights and responsibilities. A mediator will work towards helping both sides have realistic expectations so that they can work towards reaching a fair outcome together.

The mediator chairs the mediation sessions

A mediator is a facilitator and host; they will not make decisions or take sides. The mediator will establish rules to help you and your spouse follow the process and to aid productive and constructive negotiations. The agenda items for discussion will be co-created and agreed upon by the parties.

The mediator offers tools, resources, information, guidance and procedural assistance

The mediator acts as a resource provider if you need to learn about the law applicable in relation to any agenda items, the legal process and procedures. They will also refer you to other professionals, experts and online education where the need arises to support the mediation and decision-making process. For example, a referral to a 'pensions on divorce expert', known as a "PODE" to secure a pension sharing report and guidance on the importance of reviewing pension rights upon divorce. In child arrangement cases, recommendation to consider and use online parenting plan and communication tools to help parties communicate and co-parent better.

The mediator helps with exploring options

The mediator can help you look at the problems from a variety of angles and think outside the box to bring about bespoke solutions. They help you think about the issues without becoming too emotional about them. This can be important because people often get stuck in their own individual views on what is right and what is wrong. The mediator helps both parties see things from a different perspective; to step into the other parties' shoes and into their children's shoes.

The Mediator acts as an agent of reality

The role of the mediator is to help evaluate options. Act as someone who keeps things real and works towards common sense solutions that everyone feels they can live with. Mediators are there to make sure neither party goes off into unrealistic expectations or tries to take advantage of the other person. They help with reality-testing proposals and ensuring that both parties are clear on the net effect and impact of any terms proposed and agreed upon in mediation.

<u>When mediation is unsuitable</u>

Mediation may be unsuitable in these circumstances:

When an injunction order or criminal proceedings are in place due to domestic abuse concerns

An injunction order is a type of restraining order where the victim of abuse obtains a court order that forbids the perpetrator from using bad conduct and behaviour against the victim (non-molestation order) and/or compels the perpetrator to move out of the family home (occupation order) and not come within a certain distance of them for a period of time. Similar protection can be afforded via the police and criminal justice system, where criminal charges are pursued against the perpetrator.

These types of orders and restrictions are used in cases where there are grave concerns and evidence of domestic abuse, and the court is satisfied that without an order in place, the applicant's and/or their children's safety and well-being will be at grave risk of harm.

Generally, mediation isn't a good idea in these circumstances because of the power imbalance and the likelihood that the victim of abuse will be too frightened to mediate.

When there is extreme conflict, imbalance of power and concerns about lack of transparency

If there is an intense imbalance of power, the mediator may not feel comfortable giving an equal voice to both parties. This is because, with such an imbalance of power, one party may have the upper hand, for example, where one party has full financial control of family finances, and there are concerns about lack of transparency and hiding of matrimonial assets.

The mediator will not be able to redress this power imbalance, which would mean that the financially weaker party would not feel safe and possibly feel pressured into agreeing on things that will not be fair or serve them.

Where one or both parties feel coerced into attending

Mediation is a voluntary process that is intended to benefit both parties and to facilitate open and transparent negotiations. If one of the parties feels they are being coerced into attending, then that party will likely withdraw from the process, and mediation will break down.

Where the couple has already attempted mediation

If a couple has already attempted mediation with another provider that didn't work out, it is likely that a second mediation may not be successful.

One party may use problems that were never brought up to begin with in the first mediation to derail the second mediation process. When a mediator sees past issues being used as hooks to defeat the integrity of the process, they will generally withdraw from the case and close down mediation as an option.

An introduction to MIAMs

This is an initial individual Mediation Information and Assessment Meeting (MIAM) with the mediator. The mediator listens to the issues that you want to settle in your divorce and helps you determine what is essential to your case and how you can move forward with the process.

The mediator will outline the key principles of mediation and explain how it works in practice, and discuss additional dispute resolution options with you, such as arbitration, collaborative divorce, early neutral evaluation and child-inclusive mediation. This is also an opportunity to carry out a risk assessment to ensure that mediation is a safe and suitable option, given your circumstances.

On the 6th of April 2011, the Ministry of Justice issued a pre-action protocol that required anyone wishing to issue an application in the family courts in England & Wales to attend a MIAM. Currently, the other party is not required to attend, but this may alter soon with changes being proposed to the protocol to mandate both parties to attend a MIAM.

There are exceptions where there is evidence of domestic violence and/or child protection concerns, in which case exemptions will apply as set out in the section below.

The goal of this first separate meeting is to determine whether mediation is something that you may want to do. The MIAM helps both parties decide if mediation is an appropriate way forward for them. Both must agree to mediate to allow the substantive joint mediation process to begin.

In various countries, this meeting may be referred to as an 'Assessment Meeting', a 'Discovery Meeting', or an 'Information Meeting'. If mediation is assessed as safe and suitable, the parties cannot be forced to mediate against their will.

The idea behind this initial assessment meeting is that the more information you have about the divorce process, your options and other useful resources before you start your divorce journey, the better your chances of having a less acrimonious and more amicable divorce moving forwards.

What are the exemptions?

As you learnt above, mediation cannot be imposed by the UK courts, but you must provide evidence that you've attended a MIAM before issuing a court application. There are situations when exemptions will apply.

These are some of the key exemptions:

Whenever there's evidence of domestic abuse

Domestic abuse is abhorrent and is never acceptable. If this has happened to you and you're scared for your safety, then you will be exempted from having to attend a MIAM so long as you have some form of supporting evidence.

The term *'domestic abuse'* has a very wide definition under English law and covers all forms of abuse, ranging from

- Threats
- Coercive, controlling, abusive behaviour
- Psychological abuse
- Emotional abuse
- Physical abuse
- Sexual abuse
- Financial abuse
- Economic abuse
- Harassment
- Stalking
- Online and digital abuse.

There are significant child protection concerns

If there are concerns and evidence of neglect, physical, sexual, or emotional abuse of children, then mediation will not be appropriate. Where there is existing social services intervention, a MIAM exemption will apply.

The court's main concern is to make sure that the children are kept safe and protected from conflict and abuse.

You are already in the court system for the matter in dispute

If there is an existing court application in place and you wish to make a cross-application, you will be exempt from attending a MIAM.

Urgent application needs to be made without notice to the other party

If there is an imminent risk to safety or danger to life or grave and genuine concerns about your child being taken out of the country without joint parental consent, a real risk of child abduction, then you will be exempt from attending a MIAM.

You agree and wish to apply for an order by consent

Naturally, if you are looking to file a court application for an order by consent, you will not need to attend a MIAM.

Collaborative divorce

We saw that in the initial separate assessment meeting, the mediator will walk you through alternative conflict resolution options. One of these options is the *'collaborative divorce process'*.

It differs from mediation in that while in mediation, there's one neutral party (the mediator) who helps you both resolve conflicts and move forward with the divorce; in a collaborative divorce, each party engages an independent lawyer who is trained in the collaborative process. The lawyers will represent their respective clients and work together in a collaborative manner to decide how they would like to move forward with the divorce. They will have 4-way joint meetings to set the agenda and agree on issues that the parties wish to explore to reach agreement on.

The key distinction to note here is that if the collaborative process fails to support the parties in reaching agreed outcomes, then the lawyers are barred by the collaborative agreement (signed up to by lawyers and the parties) to represent their clients in any future litigation and court proceedings.

Other experts may be engaged to help and support the parties as and when necessary to act as third-party neutrals like financial planners, accountants and therapists.

A collaborative divorce is, in a way, like going to court but in an informal, less stressful setting (maybe at a neutral venue or at one of the lawyer's offices or online) where each party has their own lawyer present to protect their interests and represent them.

This process strives for a "win-win" situation for both parties, which may open you up to a fairer outcome as compared to going to court.

If you decide on a collaborative divorce, your lawyers will explain the process further and help you reach an agreement.

The main benefit of a collaborative divorce is that it avoids litigation costs and prevents negative emotions and hurt feelings from damaging your relationship with your ex-spouse, which would likely happen if you were embroiled in litigation from the get-go.

What if you can't agree? Other dispute resolution options

The ideal outcome of a mediation is for parties to agree on an amicable resolution. However, if you and your ex-spouse are unable to reach an agreement, the next step is to try other dispute resolution methods, if suitable, before going to court.

We have already explored the collaborative divorce process as an alternative dispute resolution option above; here's an overview of other primary dispute resolution options:

Lawyer led negotiations

You will need to engage and instruct lawyers to negotiate a settlement on your behalf.

They will be your mouthpiece and attempt to broker a fair settlement through direct communications between them and maybe also by arranging 4-way round table meetings.

Concerted efforts can be made on your behalf to avoid litigation and to reach agreements through lawyer-led negotiations that you both can live with.

An early neutral evaluation and Private FDR

Early neutral evaluation and a private financial dispute resolution (FDR) involve you and your ex-spouse engaging a private judge or experienced legal counsel to assess the situation and to provide you with an evaluation of how a court might determine your case.

It can be helpful in tricky financial matters or where you need to have some kind of indication of what a court might decide in your circumstances regarding difficult issues on child arrangements.

This option is usually considered and used where there is an impasse on key issues that have been narrowed by the parties, either in mediation or via lawyer-led negotiations.

An early neutral evaluation should help parties reach their own agreements by taking on board the determination and evaluation by the private judge or legal counsel, thus avoiding costly and protracted court proceedings.

Arbitration

This form of dispute resolution is the only option that provides a legally binding outcome and determination upon conclusion.

Here you and your ex-spouse agree to appoint an arbitrator of your choice to make a decision that will be final and binding on all outstanding financial and property disputes. Arbitration can also be used to resolve any ongoing child arrangement issues.

Family arbitration allows separating and divorcing couples to resolve legal disputes more quickly, confidentially and in a less formal private courtroom setting.

This forum will be tailored to meet the needs of the parties and is not governed by strict court rules and procedures, so it will be less daunting and much more flexible than litigating in court.

CHAPTER 5:

LITIGATION AS THE LAST RESORT

In all honesty, litigation and court proceedings is risky. When you think about it, you're giving a third party (a judge or bench of magistrates) who knows little about your relationship and children the power to decide how your fate will play out. It's asking them to be an involved spectator and judge in a big moment of your life, with the outcome of which could change the path of your life forever.

The judge will make a decision that will affect your financial life, that of the children and that of your property based on the applicable law and legal guidelines that don't necessarily reflect your life.

Do you want to hand over your power to make informed decisions?

Being in a courtroom is no fun, either. It's a highly stressful environment and can be very protracted and expensive. This is not what you want to deal with while going through one of the toughest times in your life. Why add unnecessary stress? What if you could make this transition into 'singlehood' as painless and stress-free as possible? Would you consider it?

Courtroom litigation poses many risks that range from financial to emotional and social, but the biggest risk of all is putting your future in the hands of a third party.

The decision to go to court can be avoided if you can sit down and talk about issues with your spouse by giving mediation a go or one of the other dispute resolution options explored in chapter 4, Mediation. You may find that you can reach mutual agreements that work for both of you.

However, if you still can't come to an agreement after months of discussion and fighting, then consider court as a last resort. Any trial can get messy and prolonged, making negotiations more complicated and expensive than they would otherwise have been. Some ex-spouses may use a courtroom setting as leverage to obtain more favourable terms during negotiations.

What litigation means in the context of divorce

A lot of things will be discussed during a trial. Everything from the division of property and finances to child arrangements, if not agreed upon and if litigated. To get a clearer picture of what you'll expect, we could categorise the issues as follows:

Issues relating to children

Can you agree on child maintenance in line with the Child Maintenance Service (CMS) guidelines, or will you need to invoke a formal child maintenance assessment in the absence of an agreement?

What will the arrangements for the children be after separation? Will there be a shared care arrangement, or will one parent be the main carer? How much time will the children spend in each parent's care? What about dividing school holidays and special occasions? All of these decisions will be made at the final hearing by a judge or bench of magistrates if not agreed.

It's at this point that you'll learn from your lawyers or mediators (or your own legal research) about the online CMS calculator as well as the law applicable under the Children Act 1989 and "the welfare checklist" that governs how the family courts decide child arrangement issues for parents. The key and paramount principle is that any arrangements should be in the best interests and welfare of the child. We will go into more detail about this area of law in chapter 8, The arrangements that have to be made.

Issues relating to finances & property division

What will happen to the family home? How will you meet your housing needs if the house must be sold and there are affordability issues? What happens to the household contents, and who gets to keep the family car? How will savings and investments be divided? Do you have a right to a share in assets that are in your ex-spouse's sole name? What are considered 'matrimonial' and 'non-matrimonial' assets? What about inherited wealth and assets? Will these be considered in the divorce settlement? What about pension-sharing rights upon divorce? How do you deal with and divide the family business? All these decisions will be determined by a judge if not agreed.

In relation to financial rights and responsibilities in England & Wales, you will learn about the Matrimonial

Causes Act 1973 and "the section 25 factors" that the court considers when determining financial rights on divorce, as well as how the court exercises its powers to make orders under the Act. The first consideration will always be the welfare of any child of the family under the age of 18.

The family courts have a wide discretion; there's no formulaic approach to sorting out finances, and each case is determined on its individual facts and merits, with the starting position being an equal share of all matrimonial assets, but this can be changed by reference to the section 25 factors.

We go into more detail about this area of law in chapter 12, Finances. It is a complex area of law. Your mediator will give you legal information and guidance on this, and your lawyer will advise you on your legal rights, entitlements and financial responsibilities upon divorce.

Issues relating to spousal maintenance

If one spouse earns more than the other and the financially weaker party is unable to meet their genuine income needs, spousal maintenance will need to be considered. Again, there is no formula to calculate maintenance awards.

Ideally, if a financial settlement can be agreed or an award can be made with a capital division in favour of the financially weaker party, which allows spouses to become independent of each other, this will be the best outcome for them. Allowing for a complete "clean break." If this is not feasible, in the absence of an agreement on maintenance provision between the parties, a judge will determine the amount of maintenance to be paid and for how long or whether maintenance should be paid on a 'joint lives' basis.

As already stated, this is a complex area of law; we will also cover this topic of maintenance in more detail in chapter 12, Finances.

Comparing mediation to litigation

In the previous chapter, we saw that with mediation, a neutral third party could help you reach an agreement in a non-adversarial fashion. Mediation usually works best if the parties have taken at least some legal advice to support the process and manage their expectations of legal rights and responsibilities.

With litigation, the lawyers for both sides take instructions from the parties to do the negotiation work on their behalf and to secure the best settlement for them. In the absence of a resolution via this method, a court application will become inevitable as both parties will now be polarised. This is where emotions get in the way.

By agreeing to mediation as the first port of call (where it is safe and suitable), you'll be able to avoid unnecessary stress, anxiety, and expensive litigation costs and save time and energy on lawyer-led negotiations and court proceedings. Litigation doesn't offer the flexibility that mediation offers, and there is no guarantee as to the outcome if it has to be determined by a judge.

The greatest benefit of mediation over litigation, and I've saved the best for last, is that since there's no determination of fault or scrutiny by a judge, the parties can stay in control of the outcomes and come to their own amicable resolutions. There's no need for hostility and animosity. Both parties can walk away satisfied with the outcome that they agreed together, and this is where the real success of mediation lies.

Comparing litigation to arbitration

Litigation and arbitration are both formal processes; however, arbitration is more flexible and is undertaken privately by joint agreement of the parties. In litigation, a judge (who the parties play no role in their selection) hears the case for each party and issues a judgement and final court order. In arbitration, the parties bring their case before a neutral third party (i.e., an arbitrator of their choice), who will hear both sides and make a legally binding arbitral award that is converted into an order by consent.

In either case, you can choose to represent yourself without a lawyer. The arbitration will be quicker than going to court to get a determination on property, finances and child arrangement issues, but the parties will need to pay for the arbitrator's service and time.

In court proceedings, there are strict rules and regulations to follow on how evidence should be gathered and presented to a judge and the preparation of court bundles in line with rigorous protocol.

There is greater flexibility with arbitrators, as you can agree on the extent of evidence to be exchanged for the purposes of determining the key issues in dispute and present your case in whatever manner is agreed as appropriate. There are no hard and fast rules and regulations to comply with, like court proceedings, and therefore it is nowhere near as stressful.

The challenge in turning a divorce into a legal event

The divorce process is mentally draining, and adding going to the court to your list of "to-dos" can make it even more stressful. Is it always necessary to go to court? While court battles are sometimes inevitable, they're best avoided if at all possible. Why?

Trials take time

While many cases don't go to a full trial, the average family law case is currently taking 12 months to conclude. The UK family court system is on its knees with a huge backlog of over 110,000 family cases, according to the statistics published by HM Courts & Tribunals Service for the period 2021/2022.

You may be required to wait for months before the case is listed for the first hearing unless it qualifies as an urgent matter that must be expedited. There are also substantial delays in listing interim and final hearing dates, adding to the protraction of the court proceedings.

When the court sets a hearing date, there is now the added stress and anxiety that your case may be pulled out of the court list at short notice due to a shortage of full-time family judges.

You'll spend a lot of time with your lawyers preparing for the case, both before and during the process. And then you'll have to do the same after each hearing and adjournment. All this means that you'll be taking extra time off work, devoting a lot of time to getting through the divorce.

It's an expensive business

If you are engaging a lawyer, you will have their fees to pay on an hourly rate - you will be billed for all the time they spend with you (in person, remotely or on calls) and in correspondence (emails and letters) and for preparation time.

You will also have court fees to pay for processing court applications, additional costs associated with hiring legal counsel if required, and disbursements for any other professionals and reports that might be needed to help resolve issues, like business valuations and pension sharing reports. However, it must be noted that such disbursements can't be avoided if required; these costs will be incurred in supporting the mediation process and other dispute resolution options too.

It's very stressful and emotionally draining

Going to court will add more pressure, stress and anxiety to your life at a time when you're already feeling down and low. This is especially true if you have to face aggressive accusations made by your ex-spouse. The children are also likely to feel the tension at school and at home.

If Children Act proceedings are issued, your child may be interviewed by a Family Court Adviser whose duty it is to safeguard and promote the welfare of children going through the family justice system. Children are likely to find this hard and may struggle to express their genuine wishes and feelings.

Staying out of court gives room to be civilised

After the divorce, you'll likely be meeting with your ex-spouse especially if you have children. Divorce can become more stressful and acrimonious, if you take up an unjustified view that your ex-spouse is trying to cheat you out of your rights. There's a danger that you'll see his or her every word or action as a way of taking advantage of you. By staying away from court, you create the best opportunity to remain civilised with each other. You'll have room to negotiate and resolve issues in your own time.

A holistic divorce focuses on compromise and discussion. Instead of fighting, you'll be working together to protect the best interests of your children and reach resolutions that are fair for you both. This will require a cooperative and non-confrontational approach on both your parts. This is easier said than done but more likely to be achievable in an out-of-court process like mediation or collaborative divorce.

<u>When litigation is absolutely necessary</u>

While most of us prefer to avoid court battles and litigation whenever possible, there are times when going to court is absolutely necessary. This will depend on the nature of your relationship with your ex-spouse and the seriousness and complexities of the issues in dispute.

We have already considered such circumstances in chapter 4, Mediation, the sections on 'What are the exemptions' and 'When is mediation unsuitable'.

These are some of those situations:

When you can't agree on how to move forward

All forms of out-of-court dispute resolution take place on a voluntary basis with the joint agreement of both parties; if there is no agreement, then the court will be your only option.

When there is a lack of transparency in financial disclosure

There is a duty on divorcing couples to exchange full, frank and honest financial disclosure to allow for an assessment of your respective financial positions for negotiations to take place on what will be considered a "fair" settlement.

If there are concerns regarding lack of transparency, non-disclosure of assets, or fear that assets may be dissipated, a court application is likely to be your best option to secure a fair outcome.

When negotiation isn't possible due to domestic and/or substance abuse

Litigation may be the only option when one spouse isn't open to negotiation or capable of fair negotiations. This is likely to be the case if you are in an abusive relationship where there is an insurmountable power imbalance or where your ex-spouse has a substance abuse problem.

In these situations, it's best to have the court decide on your behalf so that you can remain safe and avoid being taken advantage of.

When there are grave concerns about child welfare and safety issues

A court application is likely to be inevitable if there needs to be an independent assessment of any significant welfare concerns. Or when an urgent application is needed if your child is not returned after agreed contact arrangements and if there are genuine fears that your child may be taken out of the court's jurisdiction.

Preparing for litigation

Divorce can be a very traumatic time for many people. The common misconception is that you must have a stressful time with it, and many people think that the turmoil will only last several months at the most. In reality, sorting out finances and child arrangements following a separation and divorce could take up to 2 years. It is important to prepare yourself for what lies ahead, both financially and mentally.

If you end up going down the court route, how can you best prepare for litigation?

Secure the help of a specialist divorce lawyer and set up the first meeting

It starts with finding a good family lawyer that you can trust and feel comfortable with. Don't be afraid to make a number of calls to various firms and lawyers to see who resonates with you. Most law firms offer an initial free or modest fixed-fee consultation.

A good lawyer can significantly improve your chances of getting a favourable outcome. It is worth considering if they are a member of *'Resolution'*, a professional body of family justice specialists who work with families and individuals who are facing family break ups to resolve issues in a non-confrontational and constructive way. There are many lawyers out there, so you need to be thorough when choosing one. Check their reputation, experience and qualifications. It will cost you more to hire someone who is more senior, but it could save you thousands of pounds in the long run.

A divorce lawyer will advise you on your legal rights, entitlements and responsibilities regarding children and finances upon separation and divorce. They will prepare all the legal paperwork for you and communicate with your spouse's lawyer (or them directly if they choose to represent themselves) to negotiate a fair outcome in the circumstances of your case. If court proceedings are required, they will prepare the court applications and all the documents necessary to represent you in court and/or instruct legal counsel to represent you in more complex cases.

After you've settled on a respectable lawyer. Set up the first meeting. The goal of this initial meeting should be to discuss what your situation is, and what your lawyer will do for you. You need to be clear on the next steps to take and the costs associated with securing their service in both the best and worst-case scenarios so that you are prepared.

A lawyer can advise and guide you on the big-picture issues that need to be addressed in court. Their services could save you a lot of time, frustration and money, as well as emotional strain.

Get all your documentation and paperwork ready

The next step to take is to get all your documentation and paperwork ready. You should make sure that you have everything in order, sooner rather than later so that you are better prepared.

You will need the following documents and information to comply with the duty to provide full and frank financial disclosure, if you need to sort out finances:

1. A valuation of your house and any other properties that you own.

2. Details of the type of mortgages you have, and a copy of the mortgage redemption statements, including details of any early redemption penalty.

3. Estimated costs of selling any properties you own.

4. Copies of your bank statements and passbooks over the last 12 months for any bank, building society or savings accounts held in your joint or sole names or in which you have an interest.

5. Details of any investments, including PEPs, ISAs, TESSAs, National Savings, Savings Bonds including Premium Bonds, stocks, shares, gilts and securities you have, including name, type, size of holding and current value.

6. Details of any life policies, term or endowment.

7. Details of any money owed to you.

8. Details of all personal belongings that are individually worth more than £500.00 at current value, not

replacement value. For example, cars, jewellery, valuable paintings or furniture.

9. Details of any other realisable assets you have. For example, Unit Trusts, Investment Trusts, commodities, futures, and business expansion schemes.

10. Details of your debts, such as credit or store cards, bank loans, or hire purchase agreements, including the terms, total debt owed, monthly repayment and your share of the liability. Plus, details of any credit or store cards with a nil or credit balance.

11. Whether you have or may receive in the foreseeable future any other assets or financial resources not already covered.

12. Details of your pension investments, including 'the cash equivalent transfer value (CETV) for each pension or 'cash equivalent benefit value' (CEBV) if the pension is in taking.

13. A state pension forecast and valuation of additional state pension (or confirmation you do not have one). You can apply online for this information by completing Form BR19 for your state pension forecast and Form BR20 for your state pension valuation.

14. Details of your employment, including your latest P60 and last three months' wage slips.

15. Full details of all your other income from all sources.

16. Details of benefits in kind, perks or other remuneration not disclosed elsewhere received in the last and the current year.

17. An expenditure and monthly budgetary income need list if spousal maintenance is required.

18. So far as you are aware, details of the financial position of any new or intended partner.

If you have a business:

19. Your estimate of the current value, details of any possible CGT liability and the total current net value of your interest. Whether any sums are owed to you by the business. Copies of the last two years' accounts and any other document on which you base your valuation.

20. Details of any directorships you have held in the last 12 months.

21. If you are self-employed or in partnership, in addition to the last two years' accounts:

a. A copy of your last Tax Assessment but, if not available, a letter from your accountant confirming your Tax Liability.

b. Net income for the last accounting period.

c. An estimate of current net income since that date. If net incomes differ greatly, a copy of the Management Accounts since the last accounts.

The above documents will be used to complete your financial disclosure in line with court rules. This is undertaken by completing what is known as a 'Form E' and attaching relevant supporting documents to substantiate your financial declaration.

When sorting our child arrangements via the court, you do not have too much advance preparation work to undertake. Your lawyer will help you with the preparation of your court application and any other court documents and statements of evidence if directed by the court.

CAFCASS, which stands for 'Children and Family Court Advisory and Support Service', will take the lead in carrying out initial safeguarding checks and making preliminary recommendations upon an application being issued by the court.

CAFCASS represents children in family court cases in England and CAFCASS Cymru represents children in Wales. They independently advise the family courts about what is safe for children and in their best interests. They put the needs, wishes and feelings of the children first, making sure that children's voices are heard and are at the centre of the family court setting.

They carry out assessments and reports if directed by the court to prepare. CAFCASS will make recommendations upon their findings and after concluding their investigative work, which often involves ascertaining the children's wishes and feelings, in an appropriate manner according to their age and any special needs.

It will be helpful for you to keep an accurate record of key relevant events or incidents that occur regarding child arrangements, which you may wish to bring to the court's attention as evidence in support of your position. This will prove to be helpful if you are directed to file statements. It must be noted that statements of evidence cannot be filed unless you have permission from the court to do so.

Get physical and emotional support

With things moving at a rapid pace, getting therapy or professional coaching can help you come to the realisation that you need to move forward. If you can get through this period with some emotional support, it will make everything a lot easier.

One important thing to remember is that divorce doesn't affect one person; everyone involved will be impacted. It's not just about two people splitting up; it's about two families who will have to learn how to live without each other in two separate households.

If you need support in coming to terms with this, seeing a therapist could prove invaluable in helping you cope with the situation in a much healthier way than having no outside help at all.

Some of the things a therapist or divorce coach can do to help you during this time that you can't do on your own include:

- Offer emotional support and encouragement.
- Help you identify ways in which you are dealing with the situation, introspection.
- Help you cope with the stress involved.
- Help you decide how to deal with the situation.
- Hold you accountable for actions you agreed to take in a kind and compassionate way.
- Be there for you when things get tough. You might need someone to listen to your frustrations to help you get insights and clarity.

Friends and family can be a huge help as well. Having someone to talk to through this process can be invaluable, but it may not be the same as having an independent professional person supporting you.

Keeping a brave face through the whole ordeal doesn't come easy. You will want to talk to someone who can be completely objective and non-judgmental while still being someone you can trust. When you're talking with a stranger, you won't have to worry about hurting their feelings or offending them when you need someone to tell it like it is.

You should also look after your physical health to face the ordeal. This means getting some exercise and eating well so that your body is nourished and prepared for what is to come. You don't want to go into court unprepared, and feel you need time out from everything because it will only make things harder for you.

A litigated case often doesn't go to a full trial

Do you know that many litigated cases never go to a full trial? Often parties reach an agreement and settlement after court applications are issued as both come to the realisation that litigation is very costly (financially and emotionally) and time-consuming. It's not serving them or their children, and they have no control over the outcomes.

Unless there are very complex or difficult circumstances, typically, in finance cases, matters are concluded by consent after an exchange of financial disclosure or at the Financial Dispute Resolution hearing, where the judge gives a preliminary indication and views on the parties' rights and responsibilities; judicial pressure and encouragement often helps parties reach a fair resolution without going to a full trial.

In child arrangement cases, the parties often reach an agreement on future arrangements for their children after hearing from CAFCASS and considering the findings and recommendations in their report.

CHAPTER 6:

SHARING THE NEWS AND GETTING SUPPORT

After you and your partner have decided it's the end of the road, or you have come to your own conclusion or had that decision imposed on you by your spouse, it's time to tell your family and friends. How do we go about this? It's going to be a difficult and tough conversation to have. Obviously, there are many ways, and they all depend on the relationship you have with your family and friends.

In addition to telling people and breaking the news that you are separating and divorcing, there are some other steps you should take before making any statements. In this chapter, we're going to go over some of those steps and give you ideas for what to say to those closest to you.

<u>When's the right time?</u>

Legally speaking, we could say that the divorce process starts when we submit your divorce application to the court, and it starts to take effect. But practically speaking, we can say that the process began when you and your spouse started having problems in the marriage, and maybe it began even earlier when you first decided that you wanted out.

At what stage should you inform others? While this is a subjective question, and there's no single right answer, I feel that it's best to inform the children after you've had an open and honest talk with your spouse. Children are naturally intuitive. They'll start picking up on the signs and will start worrying if things don't seem right. You don't want to wait until after your spouse has moved out to tell them that this is happening and is real.

Some friends and family will be supportive; others might be hurt by your news, while some might even judge you unfairly. Be prepared for all responses.

<u>How to go about it</u>

Start by coming up with a '*separation statement*' that you and your ex-spouse can agree on. A separation statement refers to what you'll be saying to those around you when people ask about your marriage. A good statement should communicate that you're both divorcing without blaming each other and that you're doing this for the best interests of the children. It should also keep the details of your divorce private as much as possible.

A separation statement could look something like this:

"We have decided to end our marriage, and it's a decision that we've made for the best interests of our children. We will keep you updated if there are any changes in the status of our divorce. Please respect our family's privacy in these difficult times."

Telling the children that you're divorcing

It's not going to be an easy conversation to have. You might also feel a sense of guilt for being the one to break the bad news. You might be feeling powerless and angry, and you might be afraid to tell your children what's happening.

Here's how to do it:

1. Plan the time and place when you'll have the conversation with them

This won't be one of those casual conversations where you make small talk with your children and then tell them about your plans for a divorce. Planning how you'll tell them will reduce stress and make the conversation easier.

The family home is the ideal place as it's a comfortable and familiar environment. You'll want to be able to talk with them one-on-one, so try not to plan the conversation when you're expecting visitors. The best time to talk maybe during the weekend rather than a busy weekday when everyone's rushing around getting ready for school and work. They'll need time to digest the news and understand what's happening. The school breaks are an ideal time, as your children won't have to worry about missing school or having to catch up with homework, and this will also give them more time to process the news.

2. **Decide how you'll tell them**

You'll want to be honest with your children while giving them an age-appropriate explanation of what happened. A pre-schooler will need a simple and straightforward explanation of the situation, so you don't need to go into too much detail.

You might say something like:

"Mummy and daddy are getting separated because we aren't getting along anymore. We've decided to live apart from each other for a while. You will be seeing both of us regularly, and we both love you very much."

If your children are older, you might want to include a few more details about the divorce. For example, you might say:

"Mummy and daddy are getting a divorce because there's been a lot of fighting between us, and we don't want it to happen anymore. It's upsetting for all of us. We are no longer in love, but we will remain friends."

A teenager will be old enough to understand the details of what's happening, and you can talk with them about your decision to get a divorce and how it will affect their lives. You could say something like:

"Life is too short to spend it fighting with someone you don't love anymore, and I've decided to go my own way and do my own thing. I love you very much and will always be there for you, but I need some time away from your dad/mum. We're getting divorced, but we'll still be friends."

This is a time to explain the situation openly and honestly, but also to let your children know you'll be there for them when things are tough. They're old enough to understand this concept, but at that age, you still need to be careful that they don't feel rejected or abandoned. You might want to spend some extra time with them to show your commitment and love.

Older children will need to be assured that they didn't contribute to the fight and that they're not at fault. It should be clear that they'll still be able to see their dad and mum, but things will be different because the marriage is coming to an end.

Remember to keep your explanations free of blame or criticism of your spouse and only refer to his or her faults if asked directly in a neutral way. You don't want to alienate your children by pointing fingers or casting blame.

3. If it's possible, break the news together with your ex

This is not always feasible; however, if possible, do try to tell your children together. A united front is the best way to break the news to your children. It will give you the opportunity to explain the situation in more detail together, and it will help them understand that both of their parents are on the same page. Your children need to see you both as individual and separate people who still care about them and love them.

It can be difficult to be on the same page but try your best to do so anyway. The last thing you want is for your children to blame one parent over another or feel like they're taking sides when they're not. If you sense tension or anger between your ex-spouse and yourself, it might be best to break the news separately.

They'll be worried about how this will change their lives, so tell them in advance how they'll be affected and what they can expect. Most importantly, it's vital to let them know you still love them very much and that they are not to take on any blame; it's absolutely crucial to stress that this is not their fault.

4. Explain to them how things will change

Divorce changes almost every aspect of a child's life, including home and family environment, financial situation, traditions and holiday plans. If you have young children, they might need some time to adjust to the new living arrangements; always be mindful of their needs and make changes to their arrangements at a pace that they can adjust to.

Explain to your children that their routines will change and that your divorce does not mean that you love them any less. If you want to talk about the changes, start with where they'll be staying, when they'll be visiting the other parent, and how much time both parents will spend with them and reassure them that you'll work together to make the transition phase easier. Every child deserves to know that the decisions are not being made in anger but with love and good intentions.

5. Re-assure them of your love

Children are always confused when their parents' divorce. Their world has been turned upside down, and they might even feel guilty, thinking that the divorce is their fault. They might also feel abandoned in one way or another, but what you should do is remind them, again and again, that mum and dad love them to bits. Remind them that your relationship with them will never change and that the parent who does not have care of them during any given time will always be there at the end of the phone to talk about anything on their mind.

At this unsettling time for your family, it may be wise to consult with a family psychotherapist to help you all cope with the transition and change. Such therapeutic input has supported many separating couples that I have worked with in mediation to heal and transition in a much healthier way.

6. **Encourage the children to express their feelings**

It's not uncommon for children to display a range of emotions after hearing the news. You might even see them acting out in some way, like refusing to talk or eat or even crying excessively. This is common among young children because they're still learning how to express their feelings in a healthy way. If your child seems unusually quiet and withdrawn, you may need to encourage him or her to open up and talk about what they're feeling.

Let the child know that they can ask questions, and you'll answer them to the best of your ability. If they ask where daddy/mummy is or why you don't live together anymore, tell them the truth in simple terms that they can understand. You may want to assure them that their relationship with dad/mum will not change because of the divorce and that you're still a family but just in a new form.

It's wise to inform the children's nursery and school about the separation so that they can put into place additional support for your child if needed and keep a closer eye on them for you during this difficult period of transition.

<u>Telling family that you're divorcing</u>

How do you tell your family that you're divorcing? What do you say? What is the best way to break the news to them, so they don't feel let down? This is a tough one. Because your family loves you and will have strong feelings about this news, you have to find a way to tell them so that it won't hurt them too much. You also have to tell them in a way that helps you keep a good relationship with them after the divorce.

Your parents will be worried about their grandchildren, so you might want to reassure them that their needs will be taken care of as priority. If you're able to talk in private, tell them exactly what is going on.

Your father and mother might also be worried about your financial situation and all the changes that might come. To them, you're still their child, and little has changed. It might be best to reassure them again that everything is going to be alright and that you'll still provide for your children, even if you aren't married anymore.

You may want to avoid the word "divorce" when talking with your parents because it's one of those words that cause immediate alarm and distress. You can always tell them that you have decided to separate or that the marriage is no longer working instead of using the word divorce. When breaking this news, it's also important not to place any blame on them or make either of them feel like they're at fault. You don't want to isolate yourself from your nearest and dearest. You will need their support more now than ever.

Your siblings and other close family members will likely side with you on this matter, so make sure you maintain a good relationship with them and keep them close. They will be your lifeline in this difficult transition.

Telling co-workers and mutual friends

You'll want the people that you work with, who knew you as "Mrs. or Mr. Smith" to know that you're divorcing.

These people might include the HR department, managers and team members. As hard as it may be, you must tell them first because they'll need to change your title and update your surname (if reverted back to your maiden name) on employee records and other documents. Remember to keep the announcement formal - you're expected to maintain a degree of professionalism when communicating with work colleagues.

Your mutual friends are the next ones in line to hear that you're divorcing. Again, you'll want to tell them in an even-handed way and, as much as possible, avoid conversations that could turn into disagreements and taking sides. Just tell them that the divorce was unavoidable, but it will not affect your friendship.

In this modern age where social media has become a big part of our lives, you might want to consider telling your friends and relatives online. Personally, that's not for me, but many people choose to make announcements in this fashion on platforms such as Facebook and Instagram. Remember, these are public forums, and to have a dignified divorce, you should only post if you can keep the post clean and amicable. If you're not feeling that way due to the circumstances of your breakup, then I'd strongly suggest that you stay clear of social media. You don't want to put anything rude or offensive out there that you may later regret and that your children may have access to.

Here are a few ways you could word a social media post informing your friends and acquaintances of the divorce:

"After weeks of debate and careful decision-making, I've made a choice to apply for a divorce. We've come to realise that our marriage is no longer working, and we're now moving forward as two separate individuals."

"Today is a difficult day for us as we must announce that we're divorcing after 25 years of marriage. We've worked very hard to keep our relationship strong, but there are things that occurred recently that have changed all of this. We will remain friends but will now move forward with our lives separately and without each other."

"Life has its ups and downs, and sometimes things just don't work out. So, after ten years of marriage, we have decided that it's in our best interest to apply for a divorce."

"Even beautiful relationships have their ups and downs. After years of marriage, we have realised that our marriage is not as strong as it used to be. As a result, we've decided to split and move on separately."

<u>How things will change</u>

Divorce will change your life. You'll foresee the loss of a partner as your main source of emotional support in the years to come. Other family and friends will become much more important as you'll lean on them for comfort, understanding, advice and help.

The divorce will change your financial position. You may have to cut back on your lifestyle and outgoings because you'll only have one income to rely on; there will be uncertainty about your respective financial rights and responsibilities and anxiety about how you're going to cope on your own.

There's no way of knowing how you'll feel about the divorce or how your life will be altered by your new role as a co-parent. There will be a huge period of transition and adjustment.

Suppose you have a choice and the option, don't make any rash decisions in the first year after divorce, such as moving house or changing jobs that you may later regret. You don't know how long the proceedings will take to conclude. It can be around 12 months before your new identity as a single person, a *'divorcee',* is formalised via a Final Order (previously known as Decree Absolute prior to the new no-fault divorce). In some cases, it may take up to two years to finalise legal proceedings and your divorce.

In this section, we're going to go over some of the things that will change and how you can anticipate and deal with them.

If you're the one initiating the divorce, you'll deal with your feelings, accept that you're making a change and start to plan for your new life. Be mindful that the adjustment and transition will be easier and quicker for you. If you find it hard to cope immediately after the divorce, take time to grieve, which is a process of accepting and learning to live with this change in your life. You may need professional help at this stage.

If you're the spouse who's being divorced, it's important to understand that getting divorced isn't a sign of personal failure or weakness; there are many reasons why couples separate and many complex problems that can only be resolved by divorce.

Know this:

You'll become independent, and you'll start to believe in yourself

After maybe many years of collaborative decision-making and relying on your spouse for financial and emotional support, you'll suddenly find yourself on your own. This may no longer feel like a natural way of living for you. You might feel that you don't know how to live without spending time with your partner or doing things that are important to him or her. The reality is that you will adjust, and that life will be better.

You'll have more time

You'll have more time to do things that you've wanted to do; visit family and friends, plan what you want to spend any savings on, go shopping, travel, read and study.

After my separation in December 2016, I took my first-ever solo trip to Thailand in February 2019. I had the most amazing time! It was so liberating and an opportunity to find myself again, having lost my true self and identity over the years through tough and challenging times in my marriage.

You'll get back in touch with your old friends

You may have lost touch with old friends when you got together as a couple. Now's the time to get back in touch and renew your connections. Make sure you keep your old friendships - you might need them for support when you're feeling alone and in need of good company and a laugh!

You'll throw yourself into parenting

If you're the parent who has primary care of the children after divorce, you'll be focused on them more than ever before. They're the centre of your life now, and you'll be looking for ways to make up for the loss of your marriage and spouse.

You'll feel a renewed sense of responsibility towards your children since you'll be their main carer and main supporter. You'll need to feel appreciated for what you're doing now; this will help you cope with their disapproval or anger at the time of separation.

You'll get back in touch with your career goals

You may have put career goals on hold when you got married or had children, but now's the time to remember them and think about how to achieve them. I can't believe how far I've come in my own career path since separating and divorcing.

You'll feel challenged and alive again

A divorce will mark the end of an old relationship and a new start for you. You may feel sad, angry, frightened or confused. These are normal reactions to the end of a long relationship. If you don't deal with these feelings, they'll overwhelm you, and you'll feel depressed or anxious. Try to talk about how you're feeling; it will help you get through this difficult period.

Be emotionally supportive of yourself and identify your feelings, even if they change rapidly from minute to minute. Don't be hard on yourself; give yourself time to heal - it can take several months to years for your emotional wounds to start closing over.

Memories of the marriage will fade and become distant

You might find yourself remembering the good times in the marriage rather than the bad ones. Getting accustomed to being alone can take up some of your emotional energy initially. This will probably be the case whether you've lived with your spouse for decades or just a few years.

You'll have more energy for your hobbies, activities and interests

You'll probably find that extra time will let you get back into the things that you used to enjoy doing before the marriage. If you're a sportsperson, this will be a good time to restart your old sporting activities. If you belonged to a club or organisation, it can be a good time to start that again or consider volunteering.

CHAPTER 7:

THE JOURNEY THROUGH SEPARATION FROM THE CHILD(REN)'S VIEW

<u>What children need at any age</u>

Children of various ages react differently to divorce. This is because their level of maturity is not the same; therefore, their reactions and emotions are also different. Adolescents and older children can comprehend what's happened better than younger children. Most of the time, older children will understand why their parents chose to get a divorce, whereas the young ones won't.

Toddlers' cognitive skills are limited; therefore, they cannot understand what is happening. The best thing to do is to give them an explanation in the way children of that age would understand. Explain to them how your family's life will be different once their parents are divorced and give some simple explanation as to why.

Children may also think that their parents are no longer together because of them, so reassure them that this is not the case. They should be told that they did nothing wrong and are still loved by both parents.

How are infants and toddlers affected by divorce?

Their routines will become disrupted as their parent's love for them will no longer be perceived to be the same. They might feel at fault and loved less, but that is not true. They might feel angry at their parents for having gotten a divorce. Their fundamental needs, such as food, clothing and shelter, are still being met by their mother and father.

They may start asking questions about why they can't see their grandparents from the other side anymore, what happened to the toys they played with before, or why they have different clothes now. They might start crying because they don't understand, and their wants are no longer respected by their parents; this is completely normal as this is part of growing up.

A developmental delay, increased irritability, inability to concentrate and difficulty in learning are just some of the behaviour problems that can be observed in a young toddler.

Helping infants and toddlers adjust to divorce

At this age, the only thing that matters to a young infant and toddler is their mother and father and the feeling of security and love. Therefore, it would be best for you to spend more time with them by playing with them, reading stories or just spending quality time with them. The more time you spend together will allow them to feel safe, secure and wanted.

Reassure them that you still love them, and their lives will remain the same, although instead of living in one happy home with both parents, they will now have two happy homes with each parent.

You can explain to them in language that they will understand at their tender young age, that their other parent still loves them, and they'll continue to see them.

It is very important at this age for the child to have a strong bond and connection with both parents (so long as there are no safeguarding risks), as they will take this as a sign of love and will feel safe and secure.

Divorce from a pre-schoolers and a school-age child's perspective

Tough questions like, "When is my daddy coming back home?" or "Is my daddy gone for good?" can be troubling for a young child. At this age, they'll be egocentric and will likely blame themselves for their parent's divorce. Their world will feel like it's crashing down on them, and at this point, they'll need your love, attention and support.

They may also feel lonely since a significant other in their life (the parent who is not their main carer) is not around much anymore due to the divorce. Explain to them that both parents are still there for them, and even though daddy or mummy does not stay with them anymore, their love for them never changed. However, their lives have changed as they'll now be living with each parent in separate households.

You need to reassure them by telling them that they are still loved by both parents equally and that they will have a happy and fun time at both homes.

Divorce from the teenager's perspective

A teenager's critical thinking is at its peak, so it would be best to explain to them the implications and impact of the divorce. This can be done by telling them that their parents' marriage isn't stable and that parting ways is the only way to make their lives better and happier.

At this age, they might be resentful towards their parents and angry at the fact that they got a divorce; these are normal emotional responses. They will feel lonely, so spending quality time with them will help them cope better with what is happening around them.

Being provided with insight into why their parents had to separate can help ease the concerns of a teenager. Also, it is important for them to understand that getting married or breaking up is a personal choice, and there are no right or wrong answers. It all depends on individual circumstances and considerations like trust, faith, respect and money issues that may come into the decision-making.

Teenagers can understand why their life will be different, and this will help them adjust to the change better than younger children. They are likely to make their own decisions about who they want to live with and how much time they want to spend with the other parent.

Explain to them that it is not their fault, their parents remain on good terms (if indeed that is the case), and the breakup was entirely due to personal reasons and circumstances. Reassure them that they will maintain a good relationship with both parents (assuming there are no safeguarding issues).

Tell them that both parents are still there for them so that they can feel secure and loved.

What they'll learn

In a way, this unexpected transition in their lives will teach them life lessons on love, relationships, breakups and how to deal with change and loss.

Here are a few things that they'll learn during this event:

They'll learn to be resilient

Resilience is the ability to bounce back from challenges and disappointments. Although this is a tough time for the whole family, it is especially difficult for the children. Starting from a young age, they'll have to learn how to deal with this situation and dig deep to have the strength to face tough times. In other words, they'll learn how to be resilient as children as they will have to feel pain and build themselves up again.

After this event, they'll be able to take on challenges that might have seemed too hard before. They'll learn that they are not made of glass that will shatter with the slightest touch of a challenge. Consequently, they'll turn out to be resilient adults who can take on most life challenges.

They'll learn to be independent

This lesson might be difficult for children who are accustomed to always having their parents near them. However, being independent is a good thing, as they will know how to stand on their own two feet without their parents by their side all the time.

In life, they will have to face situations where they will have to stand up for themselves and deal with situations that come up on their own. This is a great life skill as it will help them develop into an independent person who can stand up for themselves whenever necessary.

They'll learn that life isn't fair

It is important to teach children how to deal with challenges when they don't come out in their favour. Life isn't always fair, and this is a fact that children who learn this at a young age will understand very well. They might not be able to do much about it, but they'll know how to face such situations and deal with the consequences. Therefore, they'll learn that life is full of ups and downs because there will be challenges every step of the way. This lesson will help them develop a stronger life philosophy, and they'll also know how to cope when things don't go their way.

Instead of playing the 'victim card', they'll understand how to deal with the challenges that life presents to them as a fighter. They might not be able to do much, but they will handle everything with a positive attitude while having patience and perseverance. This is a great lesson for children who are accustomed to living their lives based on feelings and emotions. They'll learn how to be happy in even disastrous situations, so they can turn negative situations into positive ones.

They'll learn that they'll need to be self-sufficient

Being a child, most parents are responsible for ensuring that their children are okay and provided with everything they need. However, how will they do it if the parents don't have the necessary finances? Children who find themselves in this situation will learn how to be self-sufficient and take care of themselves when needed.

They'll learn how to deal with obstacles in their everyday lives and be able to handle them on their own. They'll become strong individuals who know how to do things on their own, which will make them tough children who can face life's challenges head-on.

They'll learn that loss will come to all people, but you should never give up hope and faith. This is a hard truth for children who are accustomed to living the good life and having everything they desire. However, they'll learn that sometimes you have to accept the loss and move on, no matter how hard it is.

As parents, you should help children cope with this situation by being there for them every step of the way. You'll have to deal with your own emotions and put all your effort into helping your children through these times. Show them how you're coping and give them a strong example of how things can be dealt with in such circumstances.

<u>Do they deserve to know the truth?</u>

Should you give an explanation about what took place? This is a tough decision to make, and you need to take it into consideration. On the one hand, you need to give them the truth because they might not otherwise understand or accept the events that took place. Letting the children know why you're parting ways might lead them to cling to those things in their hearts. However, you may want them to know that it's not your fault if the other person chooses to end the marriage. That's your prerogative. If you think it will help them understand and cope with the split better, then tell them the truth in an age-appropriate manner. It's not about pointing fingers at each other or holding grudges against each other.

Depending on the situation, you can say:

"We're not getting along, and we're both so busy with our own responsibilities and other stuff that we haven't put as much time and energy together as we should have. We've grown apart and feel like it's best if we don't spend time together anymore."

Be sensitive to their feelings and give them an open-minded approach when you talk to them about the reasons why your relationship has ended.

On the other hand, you need to prepare yourself mentally as they might not accept your decision or even blame you for everything. Instead of being upset with them every time they ask questions, try answering them in a diplomatic way by saying "I love you" whenever it's needed.

Knowing how to respond to children during these difficult times is a big challenge, and it will make you feel like you're on edge. There is always going to be a series of questions that need answers. You have an obligation to provide the answers about what happened and how you ended up splitting. They might have questions like:

"How did it start?", "What was the reason?", "Why did you move away?" and "Why didn't you tell us?"

The most important thing to remember is to be genuine when you're talking with your children and tell them what you can in an age-appropriate way, honestly and truthfully. If you don't have the answers, then simply state that. You won't have answers to all their questions.

<u>When the children are used as pawns</u>

In chess, a pawn is the most important piece because it's the basic soldier that can form a part of an offensive attack or defensive strategy. When a player loses his or her pawns, it means the end of his game. After a divorce, when a parent uses the children as a way of taking you down, it's a form of betrayal that is so unfair and can cause immense pain and suffering.

A divorce can be both emotionally and financially draining, but the worst part is when one parent uses children to hurt the other parent by using them as pawns.

In what ways do divorced co-parents use children this way, and how can we avoid it?

It starts by not talking disrespectfully of the other co-parent. Sure, your ex may be unreliable, but the best way to approach it is to let the children figure that out for themselves. For instance, when it's time to talk about their other parent coming over for a visit, be sure to say it in a positive light. Don't have a negative attitude and say things like: "He better not be late like he always is." These types of negative sentences needlessly hurt the children and just build up ill feelings and resentment.

Letting the children spend quality time with their other parent is a great way to heal the wounds that were created during the divorce. Being in contact with both parents helps children understand what happened and what's going on now. The other parent can also be there to support them in their studies, social life and any other activities. Therefore, it's important that each parent spends a good amount of quality time with their children.

The children's emotional health and well-being should be at the heart of considerations when it comes to dealing with divorce. If they feel supported and understood by both parents, children are likely to heal faster from the trauma they will experience because of the divorce.

Guiding children to work through their emotions

During the divorce and after it, what emotions will your children feel?

Fear and anxiety will be the first. As they observe the adults who are supposed to provide emotional safety and security, they will begin to understand that things are not as they used to be. This is when children often feel anxious, afraid, and filled with questions about the future.

The transition of moving from one house to the other will likely contribute to this as children adjust to their new living arrangements and environments. Also, time alone in the house, new homework routines, and many more everyday tasks will all contribute to this period of change. They are just learning how to be adults in a new world. As they begin the transition from one place of security to another, the feelings that they experience set into motion a chain of questions, answers and challenges.

Anger may also be present. Children often feel angry about the changes that occur during and after the divorce.

They might not understand the reasons for the separation, their parents' new relationships or other factors from the divorce. This can result in them feeling angry toward their parents and possibly even themselves. In any case, it is essential for you to help children understand why your former spouse is no longer living with you and what it means for them so that they can overcome these feelings.

Children may also experience a sense of loneliness or sadness as they miss what was once a daily routine. They may still be unclear of their new surroundings, how things work and who to talk to. Solitude can trigger feelings of sadness and depression, which may have a negative effect on their emotional and psychological well-being.

The best way to deal with the emotions that your children experience at this difficult time is to give them the love and support they need, as well as explain to them in simple terms what is going on.

The first thing will be to help them validate their feelings. Tell them that it is okay to be sad, anxious or angry and allow them to express the way they feel. Support them so that they can overcome their negative feelings by reassuring them that everything will be okay.

Furthermore, give them the opportunity to talk about their thoughts and feelings so that you can help them come up with solutions to manage those emotions.

Also, try not to blame anyone for how they are feeling. Children are likely feeling conflicting emotions because of their parent's separation and might even blame themselves. Avoid placing accountability on your children, as it will only lead to self-blame and a sense of depression or inadequacy over time.

As the emotions and questions about their future may stem from their relationship with you, it will be essential for you to support them again by giving them the love and attention that they need. When you give your children positive feedback, love and support, it will, in turn, ensure that they can live peacefully in this difficult time.

To teach younger children to manage their emotions, start by asking them what they think characters in a movie or book feel after certain events happen in the movie or story. After they've identified character emotions, ask them to describe how they think characters might feel in a different setting. What do characters do when something terrible happens to them? How do they react? Do they think about what happened and feel sad or angry? This will help them understand their own feelings and emotions and, hopefully, express them.

Finding answers to difficult questions in advance

If there's one thing children aren't afraid of doing, it's asking the "difficult questions"- they have the innate ability to cut right to the heart of the matter, and they're not afraid to do it.

They probably asked you about Santa Claus. They probably asked you how babies are made. And they'll undoubtedly ask you why mummy and daddy don't live together anymore. If they haven't done so already, prepare yourself for those emotionally charged conversations by finding answers to these questions in advance.

Begin to tell your children that you don't know all the answers and that you only know what's going on right now. It may be difficult for parents to explain everything that's happening, but you can help children understand by repeatedly reminding them of what they do know.

Here are some of these questions:

Why did my parents' divorce? Will they divorce me, too?

After informing your children that it is not their fault, help them understand that people separate when they no longer love each other or have problems in the relationship that they cannot sort out and are making them both unhappy.

If you think your child is ready to understand this, try teaching them a simple explanation of the word "divorce." You can say, for example: "Jack and Jill love each other very much, but sometimes two people stop loving each other and want to live apart. When this happens, we call it divorce."

Explain how their life will soon change and that they'll need to adjust to new living arrangements and routines. Emphasise that both parents love them so much and that they'll love them even more in the future; parents do not divorce their children.

If you feel that they're not quite ready, you can explain and say something like: "Mummy and Daddy are still going to see each other, but we need to live in different places for a while."

Can I fix it?

Older children will probably listen to the divorce news and think they've done something wrong. As they try to figure out what went wrong, they'll begin to seek ways to "fix" the situation.

To help them understand that their parents' problems are not their fault, you can explain that you and your ex-spouse had many unhappy times together, and while you both tried, there was nothing you could do to make things better.

Remember that as much as children want their parents back together, a divorce is usually a permanent choice. Instead of explaining how things are going to be "fixed," teach them about change by showing them that for every problem, there's a solution.

Will you stop loving me like you stopped loving mum/dad?

This question won't usually be brought out of the blue. After they've misbehaved or done something mischievous, they'll probably ask you this question. It's a way of testing the limits, and they're trying to make sure you still love them.

Reassure your children that divorce doesn't mean that either parent loves them less. "I will always love you, no matter what" is a great response to this question. You might even want to say, "Mummy and daddy still have love and respect for each other because we had you."

When talking to your children about divorce, just remember that the more you prepare, the easier the conversation will be. Anticipating your children's questions and keeping your answers simple will also help. Remember, your children are probably scared, confused and looking for reassurance that they'll be okay. Give them all the love and reassurance you can.

Keep a positive attitude and explain that life is still good, but sometimes people grow in different directions, and they want to go their separate ways. As much as you want to explain the details of what happened, don't attempt to cover too many complex issues at a time. Letting things sink in slowly will help your children adjust to the new way of life.

CHAPTER 8:

THE CHILD ARRANGEMENTS THAT HAVE TO BE MADE

In this chapter, we'll look at child arrangements that parents must try to reach an agreement on when contemplating a split. *'Child arrangements'* is the term used under English law to describe where a child lives and how much time the child spends with each parent. A *'parenting plan'* can be drafted to reflect the arrangements agreed upon for the children setting out in detail how the parents will each care for the children and meet their needs.

A "child arrangement order" will be pursued if agreements on child arrangements cannot be achieved between parents following a separation. This replaces the old "residence order" and "contact order." The legal basis for a child arrangement order is under section 8 of the Children Act 1989. Prior to this legislation, the terminology used was "child custody" and "child access" - these terms are now obsolete, but people often still refer to these outdated terms when talking about child arrangements.

The options for sorting out child arrangements

Many parents agree on the terms of their separation before they get divorced. For example, they may decide on an equal distribution of time with their children and that both parents will share responsibility for costs associated with their upbringing and their educational expenses.

A mutual agreement refers to when the two parents come together and decide on a child arrangement themselves. The more popular arrangement these days is on a "shared care" basis, with the parents dividing up care and responsibility for the children on an equal or near enough equal basis.

However, in many cases, divorce is an emotionally charged event, and it's far from easy for parents to come to an agreement about the future of their children. Sometimes matters aren't so straightforward, and one parent is likely to feel that his or her ex-spouse's requests are unreasonable or unfair.

If the parents can't agree, the first port of call should be to consider mediation or other dispute resolution options (unless exempt) as discussed and explored in chapter 4, Mediation and chapter 5, Litigation as a last resort. If that fails to resolve the matter, then a court application for a child arrangement order will be inevitable.

Where child maintenance cannot be agreed upon, it is likely that the party seeking financial support will invoke the services of the Child Maintenance Service to calculate the amount payable and to enforce their rights to receive financial support for the benefit of the children in their care.

Deciding where the children will live and "the welfare checklist."

Under existing English law, the starting position is that both parents have a right to maintain a meaningful, loving relationship and close bond with their children, so long as it is safe, and in the child's best interests and welfare. As already stated, these days, more parents wish to secure a shared care arrangement to play an equal role in their child's upbringing, where this is practically feasible.

When deciding on child arrangements, if the parents can't agree, the court's paramount consideration will be the welfare of the child. The judge or magistrates will evaluate several factors known as "the welfare checklist" (not in any order of hierarchy) to reach a determination as set out here:

- The ascertainable wishes and feelings of the child concerned (considered in the light of their age and understanding).
- Their physical, emotional and educational needs.
- The likely effect on them of any change in their circumstances.
- Their age, sex, background and any characteristics that the court considers relevant.
- Any harm that they have suffered or are at risk of suffering.
- How capable each of their parents, and any other person in relation to whom the court considers the question to be relevant, is of meeting their needs.
- The range of powers available to the court under this Act in the proceedings in question.

Suppose a court's help is requested in the absence of agreeing on a parenting plan and your own child arrangements. In that case, it will make an order that it deems appropriate, and in the child's best interests considering all the above factors and the circumstances of your situation.

Coming up with a contact schedule and parenting plan

Making a parenting plan is one of the most important things you can do to ensure a smooth transition for your children. Although similar in many ways, each family is unique, and it is important to structure your parenting plan in a way that works for your family. In doing so, you may want to consider a contact schedule to help achieve shared care arrangements while striving to meet the essential needs of all family members.

Let's go over a few parenting plan options so that you and your ex can choose one that works for your family:

1. **An alternative weekly routine**

With this approach, the children spend a week with one parent and then the other on an alternative weekly basis. This routine is ideal for families with older children with busy school schedules or when the parents live a considerable distance apart.

As the weeks are alternating, it's possible to ensure that the children have a weekly routine. Regardless of which parent they spend time with, they will know what to expect and how they are being treated. This can help children develop a sense of security, predictability and trust in both parents in an arrangement that is free from confusion and distress.

2. A 2-2-3 schedule

The first two days of the week are spent with one parent, the next two with the other, and the weekends are alternated so that the children spend time with each parent on an alternative weekend basis. A 2-2-3 schedule is a good alternative to a weekly routine if there are older children that have extracurricular activities.

The advantage of this routine is that your children get lots of quality time with each parent on a more regular basis when it's convenient for everyone involved. However, make sure to take into consideration your child's school schedule and activities because their routine is important too.

You may wish to schedule a monthly one-on-one meeting with your ex to give you both the opportunity to discuss matters related to the children, such as how they are coping with the transition, progress in school, discipline and planning, so everyone is clear on arrangements moving forwards.

3. One parent with primary care of the children and another parent spending regular time with them

Here, one parent is the main carer for the children but with the children spending regular agreed periods of time with the other parent.

The advantage of this arrangement is that it allows parents to create a very clear routine for the children as well as time to themselves. For example, if one spouse has five days a week, they can plan their activities and outings accordingly. However, both parents need to be on the same page regarding how they want to work together in this fashion, or it might backfire and cause conflict between them and/or their children.

The child has the stability of one main home base with the resident parent but also the security of spending regular quality time with their other parent.

In these circumstances, there will usually be an agreement for the non-resident parent to pay child maintenance to the resident parent to help meet the financial needs of the children.

Child maintenance

As a parent, you may feel obligated to help your child financially whether or not you have care of them. As their parent, you have a legal responsibility to provide for them and to ensure that they are taken care of.

A child means someone who's under 16 or under 20 if they're in approved education or training.

Child maintenance in a shared care arrangement is effectively shared by the nature of these arrangements. Each parent takes sole responsibility for meeting the day-to-day financial needs of the children when in their care. It is normal to agree to share the costs of any larger expenditure and big-ticket items for the benefit of the children, such as school trips, extracurricular activities and expensive purchases like laptops.

Where there is one primary carer, child maintenance is payable to them by the non-resident parent in line with the Child Maintenance Service (CMS) guidelines. The website has an online calculator to help parents reach an agreement on making voluntary arrangements.

If child maintenance is not paid on a voluntary basis and cannot be agreed upon, the primary carer will need to invoke the services of the CMS to carry out a formal assessment and enforce payments.

You might have to go to court to arrange maintenance if the non-resident parent:

1) lives outside the UK or
2) earns more than £3,000 a week, and you want to top up the maintenance you secure through the CMS.

You'll also have to go to court to ask for more maintenance if you have to pay for extra things like the cost of your child's disability or education. This is because the CMS doesn't take these extra costs into account in its calculation.

Letting the children know about the new arrangements

After discussing a parenting plan and a contact schedule with your ex-spouse and reaching an agreement or, in the absence of an agreement, a court making a child arrangement order, you will have to let the children know about it. Be prepared for the possibility that they may have mixed feelings about the new arrangements. Your child may find it hard to adjust to this new childcare arrangement and prefer a different one.

If you have agreed to arrangements, you may find it helpful to have a written parenting plan to formalise the arrangements agreed upon and to share with your children. The Children and Family Court Advisory and Support

Service (CAFCASS) website is a fantastic resource for separating parents and has an excellent parenting plan template that you can use for free.

To get your children comfortable with their new arrangements, explain how they are going to have time with each of their parents in a way that makes sense for them. If you are using a calendar as part of your parenting plan, show them how they will be spending time with each parent during different weeks or months. To help your child better visualise what's happening, ask them what special things happen at certain times of the year, like holidays or birthdays. Then, let them know how they will be spending time with each parent during those times.

Don't forget to explain how this arrangement is for their benefit, not yours or your ex-spouse's. Your primary goal is to make sure that your children have a positive relationship with both parents. Be open about your feelings and any concerns you have; listening to each other can help you resolve them.

Finally, once you've come up with a parenting plan (or you have a child arrangement order), you may wish to share this with key people who are involved in your child's care to help support them and you through this transition. For example, let your parents know what the new plan or order is. Regardless of what you decide as a parent or what the court orders, you must remember to let your children know, above all, that they are loved no matter what.

CHAPTER 9:

ANTICIPATING CO-PARENTING CHALLENGES

Co-parenting after divorce is never an easy task. Sometimes, it can be even more challenging in comparison to parenting solo. There will be times when you will feel frustrated with your co-parenting partner, especially if they are not meeting your expectations. Introducing new partners and step-siblings is another major challenge when it comes to co-parenting after divorce.

Before you proceed with co-parenting, it is important for you to understand that this will be a gradual process that will require intensive effort and time on both your parts. In this chapter, we're going to go over some of the challenges that co-parenting brings along and give you some ideas on how you can improve it.

<u>Parental alienation</u>

Parental alienation is a term used to describe the deterioration and estrangement between parent-child emotionally, psychologically and/or cognitively. Even though parental alienation can be observed in both divorced and intact families, it is evident that most of the occurrences occur after a breakup. It could be because of various reasons, one of which is that the child sees their parent being replaced by a step-parent. Sadly, there are times when one parent deliberately seeks to make their child choose sides against the other parent due to a personal grudge.

Exes with extreme narcissistic tendencies or borderline personality traits are more likely to behave in this way. We could blame the parents for their children's alienation, but it is also important to find out the underlying causes and think of ways to solve them.

When one parent makes a deliberate attempt to alienate the other, it is essential to watch out for warning signs because this is when a problem becomes more serious.

Here are some of the things that you can look out for:

The children appear to be rude and ungrateful towards the alienated parent

When a child feels that one parent is on their side and the other isn't due to alienation tactics, they will begin to show signs of disrespect towards the alienated parent. They may even blame that parent for some wrong they have experienced, regardless of whether it was intentional or not.

The child has no interest in spending time with their alienated parent

As a result of alienation, your child may even stop calling or visiting the alienated parent on a regular basis. The child might think it is a waste of time since their mother or father will never accept them.

When one parent uses *"gaslighting"* to create mistrust, it is not uncommon for children and exes themselves to succumb to this type of behaviour. Gaslighting is when one party manipulates another consistently and usually over a period, to make the other party question their own reality and the true factual position. Therefore, it's important that you observe and monitor your child's behaviour carefully so as to keep an eye out for any signs of gaslighting.

When the child undermines the alienated parent's authority

Rebellion and inequality are common characteristics of narcissistic parents, so it will not be surprising if your child behaves in such a way. However, this does not mean that you can allow your child to defy and disrespect you. It is important to keep them in check so that they show respect towards the alienated parent. This can be done by keeping a close eye on the things they do and say, especially those things that have little or no justification behind them.

To counter parental alienation, it is vital that you take the right actions. One of which is to focus on open communication with your children. This will help you spend time with them and build trust as well as a good relationship.

You should also be aware of situations that could be a result of parental alienation or condemnation, and it's best that you talk to your ex-spouse about this so that they know what they're doing is not acceptable.

Talking to a therapist who is a specialist in this area is another thing you can do. This will help get rid of internalised anger and support you to get on better with your ex-spouse, as well as give you tools, tips and techniques on effective communication in such circumstances.

Holding a grudge against your ex

Another co-parenting challenge that you're likely to experience is the feeling of hatred and disgust towards your ex-spouse. This could be especially hard to cope with if you despise the things they did to you during the relationship. There is no doubt that hating and resenting your ex-spouse will make you feel angry and frustrated. But remember, doing this will also make it hard for you to co-parent with them. You may end up acting like a bitter person, and it will reflect on the parenting relationship you have with him or her.

After a divorce, it's only natural that we'll react to our ex in differing ways. Some of us may take longer than others to heal from the trauma that divorce can bring. This is because we all have different experiences to draw on when it comes to time for us to accept the end of our marriage. The anger and resentment that you feel can come out in different ways, and you may find it difficult to resist the urge to act out on these feelings. The problem with this kind of mentality is that your reactions won't be directed towards your ex-spouse, but instead, they'll likely get directed towards your children.

One way to let go of your anger is to forgive all the wrongdoings of your ex. When you've forgiven them, you'll be less likely to use them as an excuse for your actions.

You may believe that forgiving your ex-spouse will only mean that you're giving in to the person who caused all this hardship and pain, but in reality, it will help you in the long run. You'll become a stronger person, take ownership and responsibility for your own actions and take chances, which can lead to better opportunities down the line. The net effect of this is that you'll be able to parent your children with more love and strength than before.

Never bad-mouth your ex in front of or to the children. This is another way that can make you appear bitter, and it won't help issues if your children associate their dad or mum with anger and hate. Children need stability from both of their parents, so they'll be more likely to choose the parent they feel more comfortable around.

You should also be careful of the things you say to your children about your ex-spouse. If you have no respect for them, chances are that your children will behave the same if they're forced to live with them. You should not talk about how badly you've been treated or how awful their dad or mum was to you. This just gives the children ammunition against your ex, which can only make things worse for co-parenting in the long run.

Co-parenting with a narcissist

What happens when you have a co-parenting relationship with someone who has narcissistic tendencies? A narcissist's sole purpose in life is to get their own way. This can be very exhausting to deal with because they will not hesitate to use any tactic that they can think of to get their way.

It's a good idea to establish a set of ground rules and boundaries right away. These rules should be agreed upon by both parents and must be strictly followed. One good example is that the time and place of contact arrangements must be decided by both parents beforehand rather than doing it on the spur of the moment. This helps avoid unnecessary confrontations, which tend to happen when these issues are brought up at short notice.

Narcissists can be very intelligent and manipulative. They may butter up to the children or try to convince them that the things that they're doing are right. Again, you must set clear rules on this issue before any children are involved in the decision-making that the parents have together.

You should also be more understanding of your ex-spouse's views if you do have a narcissistic co-parenting relationship because they can become very aggressive unless they feel like they're getting their way. Narcissists are unable to stand losing control, and when this happens, they will resort to attacking you with verbal abuse and arguments.

By learning about the techniques narcissistic exes use to manipulate you, such as gaslighting, where they consistently deny the existence of certain things you know to be true, you can learn how to avoid falling into these traps. If a narcissist is not able to get their way indirectly, they'll either turn aggressive or ignore you altogether.

When it comes to time for children to adjust to the fact that their parents are no longer living together, it would be best if they could have the support in place to do this more easily. Narcissists are the opposite of compassionate people, so they will have little understanding of the struggles their children will face with this transition. It's important that parents who have a narcissistic co-parenting relationship have patience and try to work as a team so they can help their children through this period.

Competition between two parents

When you're dealing with two parents who want to be the best parent, there's always bound to be rivalry between them. This is something that can easily become a competition between the two of them, and it can be dangerous if they get carried away with it.

It's normal for most parents to compete against each other as they're doing their very best in raising their children, but there have to be certain limitations. What happens when these limits are pushed too far?

After a divorce, the first thing that usually goes is the friendship between the two ex-spouses. This can seriously affect how your children will experience growing up and can also affect how you and your ex will be able to co-parent together.

Competition between parents is dangerous for children because it usually causes them to become caught up in their parents' emotional conflicts. This kind of environment is not healthy for children because they tend to blame themselves for what happened between their parents.

It's a good idea if you can address issues like this early, before things get out of hand.

To counter this challenge, make rules and set boundaries about the kind of gifts you can buy your children and other activities you can do together as a family. This way, the competition will not be as harsh between the two parents and should be more enjoyable.

Parallel parenting

We've seen that a winning parenting plan is one that permits both parents to feel respected and appreciated and for co-parenting to work, both parents need to feel like they can offer input and give advice on parenting. We've also seen that we all want to feel important and that feeling cherished by your children is a primary part of feeling important. So, how can we make co-parenting work in a situation where the exes are unable to get along, perhaps due to the greater reasons that contributed to their divorce?

Parallel parenting is in many ways similar to co-parenting: They're both effective approaches for dealing with the reality of divorced parents. However, there's one important difference between them, and this is that with parallel parenting, communication is kept to a minimum, with each parent having autonomy on how they will exercise their joint parental responsibility when the children are in their care. Each parent utilises whichever parenting approach they feel works best for them in their situation, knowing that the other parent will also do the same.

In a parallel parenting approach, both parents are taking responsibility for their children, even though they may not both attend the children's school events or spend time with the children at the same time of day, or even go to some functions together. It's not realistic to expect all parents to do that, and so this concept allows you and your co-parent to focus on what you can both do for your children in your own way.

The idea is that both parents are willing to agree on a certain number of areas in which they'll both be involved in their child's upbringing separately from one another, and then each parent will work on diligently implementing those agreed-upon responsibilities.

The challenge that parallel parenting solves

In highly volatile divorces such as one where domestic abuse led to the marriage break up, it wouldn't be far-fetched to say that the exes may not be able to agree on anything.

When this happens, then what to do?

Parallel parenting is a good way of dealing with this dilemma because it allows each parent to feel like their input is valued, their concerns are taken seriously and their desires for the children are taken care of. This is achieved by allowing each parent to go about raising their child in ways that are suited to them.

On the one hand, it may also be argued that by doing this, the parents could be setting themselves up for another breakdown in communication when one parent feels ignored or undervalued (which would likely happen). To combat this, the only communication permitted is that concerning the children, and even then, it's best-kept official. Writing and sending emails or WhatsApp messages is best because both parents can keep the communication formal.

Better still, make use of parenting Apps like '*Our Family Wizard*', '*AppClose*' or '*2houses*', which allow for safe and secure communication between separated parents with useful tools and resources for effective co-parenting and parallel parenting, reducing confusion and conflict.

Parallel parenting is suitable where other approaches to parenting after divorce don't work. In fact, parallel parenting is sometimes the only way of successfully continuing to co-parent after separation in many cases.

CHAPTER 10:

CO-PARENTING

Co-parenting is often a natural part of parenting after divorce, and it requires that both parents work together as a team towards the same goal: raising their children in such a way that they'll live happy, healthy lives post their parents' separation and/or divorce. Co-parenting is a form of parenting that sets out to ensure that sensible solutions are found so both parents can feel like they're making a meaningful contribution to their child's life, even if they're not sharing the same roof or bed.

What makes co-parenting so good is that it enables both parents to work together as a team, even if they're splitting up. This makes it possible for both parents to gain an insight into how their respective parenting styles differ, which means they can adapt their parenting methods to suit each other. Working together in this way also means that when the children need looking after at one parent's home or when one parent needs assistance with something at work, then both parents can offer support.

In this chapter, we'll consider co-parenting and how it makes life easier for everyone. We'll also offer a few tried and tested tips on what you can use if you feel like your ex-spouse is trying to sabotage the co-parenting arrangement that the two of you have worked so hard to agree.

However, before we get started, you'll need to know what co-parenting is.

What is co-parenting?

Co-parenting can be enjoyable for both you and your ex. It's when two parents work out how to share responsibility for the upbringing of their children both inside and outside of the home with each other. It includes decisions about their arrangements, how much time the children spend with each parent during school term and holidays, how to address a disagreement, and how to raise them if one of you is unable to provide care in the future due to, say, ill health or incarceration or any other circumstances that might affect your ability to provide care. In short, co-parenting is what it sounds like: it's co-parenting.

The benefits to children

At the centre of the concept and practice of co-parenting are the children. When parents work in partnership, their children benefit from a close relationship with both parents; it also helps them to have more stable and secure lives. This can be an enormous help to a child who is going through a difficult time when one or both of their parents are struggling with an addiction to say, alcohol or drugs. It also helps to ensure that even if something happens to one parent, the other parent will still be there for the children.

Co-parenting provides stability and reduces stress. The divorce process will be stressful for children who may not be able to grasp the concept of why their parents are separated. Co-parenting provides a stable environment in which the children can start to make sense of things.

At the same time, co-parenting provides an opportunity for parents to collaborate and resolve issues regarding discipline and parenting. It's easier on children when they see that it's okay to disagree with one another or have different opinions or preferences and be willing to compromise.

Again, the children will feel secure knowing that they have a strong relationship with both parents and can freely confide in them. This is often needed when the children are going through an anxious or difficult time. They'll also know that their parents will be there to support them in getting through these tough and challenging times.

Another benefit to children is that co-parenting can help parents establish clear boundaries so that they are better able to avoid situations in which children might be harmed or manipulated. Collaboration between parents also benefits them. Both will feel valued and acknowledged in the important roles that they each play in the children's upbringing.

What are some of the challenges?

Co-parenting has its challenges, all of which can be overcome if you work together and communicate effectively.

The first challenge is that you and your ex-spouse may be in different places emotionally when you are trying to co-parent. You may not be able to see the world from your children's perspective and make decisions about their lives that you know they will disagree with. This means that sometimes you'll have to step back for a moment and evaluate what the best decision is for your child.

Also, co-parenting can mean working through issues about finances and creating a parenting plan. Think of it as two people having their own ideas about how to run their household - along with how they would like the household to look and function - but who also want their children to feel included, safe and happy. It can feel like a lot of work, but it is worth it.

Another challenge is that it takes time for parents to adjust to the 'new normal'. They might have a hard time with their child spending more time with the other parent or having less time together. And from the child's perspective, it can feel strange going from seeing a parent every day to not seeing that parent for a period. This can be an enormous adjustment, but it is also one that will help strengthen your relationship with your children in the long run. To the children, it means having both parents as a strong presence in their lives, not just one parent.

One of the biggest challenges for co-parenting is being able to communicate effectively with each other. The most important thing to remember is this: always be respectful and courteous, and no matter how upset you feel, try to avoid taking those feelings out on your ex. Doing so will only make things worse. Instead, take a breath, pause and think before you speak or act. This can work like magic. You might even want to write things down so that you don't say something mean or embarrassing that you may later regret.

If either parent moves on and gets into a new relationship, it can be even more challenging to keep the lines of communication open and to work together. It's important for you two to make sure that tensions are not increased in this area and to understand that each of you has a right to move on. It's in your children's best interests that you all try to get along or at least be civil and polite.

Making it work

What are some of the ways we could make co-parenting work? Here are a few tips:

Communicate better

First, you have to focus on being flexible. Life is not about being right or wrong; it's about getting along and co-parenting without a child feeling like they are caught in the middle of a conflict between their parents. The best way to make this work is to keep lines of communication open and transparent, even if you are mad at each other over something - it might be better to address that problem when cooler heads prevail.

Second, be willing to compromise and let go of ultimatums. You might think that to get your way, you need to be aggressive, but if you try being kind and understanding first, chances are your ex will see your point of view as well.

Over two-thirds of marriages that end do so because of communication problems. Building a successful co-parenting relationship is about improving the communication between you and your ex-spouse. It will help you understand each other better and make better decisions for the child's benefit. How can that be done?

Start by setting the right "tone"

By tone, we're referring to the language and attitudes you use. If one of you is being defensive, the other could respond in like terms which lead to an escalation of conflict. Instead, adopt a neutral, business-like manner and attitude.

Focus on what's best for the child

Your needs and wants might get in the way of this but try to remember that your child is watching you - make choices that are not just about you but also about how you can help your child be happy. You can't control everything that happens with your ex-spouse, so try to focus on your role as a parent instead of getting caught up in thinking about what you can do to make things more difficult for them.

Have a "no problem" attitude toward your ex's new partner

The children will more easily accept a new adult in their life if they see you getting along with them. Even if you feel like your ex-spouse's new partner is not the right person for them, keep that to yourself.

Don't play your child against the other parent

For example, don't boast about one parent over the other, compare parenting styles or try to convince your child that one parent is better than the other; this only serves to upset your children.

Focus on being a "good parent" and not a child's friend

Let go of what happened before the separation and refocus on how you can be there for your children as their parent and their role model now, as well as in the future.

Keep everything documented

Co-parenting with an ex-spouse is a lot easier when you're on good terms, and both of you want to work together to do what's best for the children. But it's much more difficult when one of you doesn't care about the children and just wants to get your own way.

When things go wrong, it helps to have a paper trail of what happened, when it happened, who was there and what was said. A notebook or diary can be a good place to jot down details, questions and answers that come up between meetings. It's also helpful to take photos at events or school functions as a way of documenting your children's growth over time.

Keep an open mind

When one parent tries to enforce his or her way, that can irritate the other parent and make co-parenting harder. Instead of reacting and becoming outwardly irritated, do the best that you can to be understanding of what they want. At the same time, make sure they are not doing anything harmful or hurtful to get their needs met above yours. Make requests instead of making demands.

It's time to think about making the co-parenting relationship work. Your children will be better off if you can stop fighting and start working together.

By staying open-minded and understanding of your different needs, working together will go much more smoothly for the benefit of all of you. You might find that your relationship with your ex-spouse improves, which may inspire mutual trust and respect and will help you co-parent better in the future.

Don't pick fights over small things

If both parents are committed to co-parenting and working together, they can do well by not letting small things that irritate escalate into bigger problems. If one parent has a problem with the other, that should be expressed and confirmed as just that - a small thing.

If something goes wrong and you can't agree on what happened, think about whether it's really good for your child to have you at each other's throats. Sometimes it's best to agree to disagree or acknowledge you're at fault. Does it help the children to have parents arguing? If you both admit that you're wrong, your child will learn the importance of acknowledging mistakes and not trying to pretend they didn't happen. They'll also see that 'parents working together' is a huge part of how separated families are supposed to function.

<u>Collective decision making</u>

There will be major decisions to be made by both of you. Decide how you're going to make these decisions together.

For example: If you are going to take the children on holiday together, decide when and where to go, how many days off you'll need from work, as well as who's going to pay for what.

Decide who is going to do what in terms of planning, booking tickets, searching destinations and coming up with different options for locations and activities.

Co-parenting needs commitment from both parents to work together as a team. The parents should be good role models at home, at work and in front of their children's friends. Credit must be given to parents who put the work and effort into co-parenting effectively as they are modelling for their children a successful break-up, which builds confidence in the parties and their children.

You continue to share parental responsibility for your children even after divorce and separation for all major areas in your children's upbringing. Of course, the usual day-to-day routine decisions can be made unilaterally when the children are in your sole care. However, for any major decisions like medical intervention, change of location or deciding on education and schools, you will need to make joint decisions.

In the absence of a joint agreement on such key areas, you should first seek the assistance of a family mediator unless one of the exemptions applies that we covered in chapter 4, Mediation. If a resolution cannot be reached with the support of a mediator, you will need to ask the court for help to determine the issue in dispute by seeking either a 'specific issue' or 'prohibited steps' order and in some cases, both depending on the circumstances.

Financial issues will also need to be sorted out. Will there be a joint bank account set up to meet the children's financial needs? If not, both parents will need to discuss and agree on who's going to pay for what.

The above areas are just some of many that parents might come into conflict over. The key is to recognise that there is more benefit in working together than trying to go it alone in a quest for personal power and control over the children and their belongings.

Diffusing high-tension situations

Let's say that your ex-spouse comes with their new girlfriend or boyfriend to the drop-off or pick-up point where you do the handovers. You might feel uncomfortable around this new partner or resentful that your ex is moving on to another relationship so soon after the divorce. The best thing to do is to keep conversations positive and brief. This is just one of the many things you'll need to work out together in order to figure out how to get along.

Create boundaries and set roles for yourselves when it comes to the children, their activities and child maintenance.

It's crucial that parents who are co-parenting know how to make the other feel comfortable when it comes to parenting time. Setting aside a designated time for each parent for special times with the children will help both of you to enjoy a sense of security about your role in your children's lives. Talk about how you're going to handle situations such as holidays, sports activities and other events that you want or need your children to be involved in.

Whenever you find yourself in a situation where you're under a lot of stress, take a few deep breaths in order to calm your nervous system before you say or do anything.

Regardless of the problems that you and your ex-spouse have had in your relationship, you still need to be able to put aside your differences and work together towards the common goal of raising healthy, happy children.

Supporting each other emotionally and discussing the principles of effective parenting will help both parents gain a holistic perspective. This involves prioritising the well-being of your children by putting aside personal feelings towards each other. By doing so, both parents can collaboratively make decisions that are in the best interest of their children.

<u>Co-parenting in public spaces</u>

What are some of the public situations divorced co-parents find themselves in? Dropping off and picking up the children at their ex-spouse's house, grandparents' and friends' houses is one. You may both meet at after-school activities like music lessons. Attending sports events, dance and school functions that the children are involved in will be another. You must be able to show that you're respectful of each other and can work together as a team so that the children don't feel ignored, excluded or embarrassed by your behaviour.

In these situations, setting suitable boundaries, being mindful of what's appropriate to say or not say, and establishing ground rules for the children will all help assure that the children see both their parents as adults who are capable of functioning together in a positive and productive manner.

Co-parenting in public spaces includes turning up on time and being prepared when you're meeting with your ex. You need to show that you are responsible, dependable and reliable.

The end game of working hard at co-parenting is to be able to share space with your ex and the children in all key milestones of their life. To share in future special occasions and celebrations like their first day at school, their 10th birthday, their graduation, their marriage and the birth of grandchildren.

Children should not feel like they are caught up in parental conflict for the rest of their lives. They should not have to choose which parent to invite to special occasions and celebrations as they get older. This will not be fair on them, you, or your ex-spouse.

Having put into practice these words of guidance, my ex and I have shared key milestone celebrations since our separation and divorce, like both children's graduations. It's great to be able to share space without any animosity, and have a good time as a family together, even after parting and going our separate ways.

We must take the lead and responsibility in modelling happier, healthier lives post-separation and divorce for ourselves, our children and future generations.

PART 3:

AFTER THE DIVORCE – HEALING

CHAPTER 11:

ADJUSTING TO THE NEW LIFE

<u>What will it be like after the divorce?</u>

Life after divorce has its fair share of struggles: Having dinner alone, challenges when co-parenting, losing the mutual friends that you had with your ex, and wondering when you'll ever meet someone again. However, once you get over the initial grief and pain of divorce, there is a new life waiting for you.

One of the surprises that comes with this newly found freedom is the ability to do all the things you never had time or energy to do before. A lot of divorced parents end up rediscovering parts of themselves that they had left behind, such as hobbies and interests.

There will also be new things you'll discover that you like. It's a chance to try new activities such as pottery classes or going to the gym. You'll have the opportunity to start taking care of yourself in ways you would never have done before, eating better and exercising regularly. This can be a great opportunity to inspire your children by leading by example.

You're now the head of the household

If you are the parent with primary care of the children, this means that you'll be the one they will look up to and give their absolute trust and respect. Adjusting to this new life of being a single parent and being responsible for the care and well-being of your children might seem daunting at first, but it's what you need to do. It doesn't matter how old the children are; infants, toddlers, teens or adults - they look up to you and respect you.

As you're getting used to your newly assigned role of being the main carer, you'll see that the most important thing right now is to manage your well-being and that of the children. Balancing work, childcare and time with your children - it takes a lot of effort and dedication. And the only way to do that is to make sure you're taking good care of yourself. You must fill your own cup first when it comes to care, so that you have the capacity and energy to then care for your children and others

You are likely to come across these single parenting struggles and parenthood dilemmas that you should expect:

Loneliness

In a way, this is more of a single-parent struggle than a parenting one. The loss of a partner can make you a lot of things; lonely, sad, depressed and so on. But you shouldn't let that define who you are. Some past experiences that have made you who you are aren't going to go away overnight. They might feel like they do, but they're not going to disappear just because your partner is no longer in your life. So, instead of letting them make you feel miserable, embrace them and enjoy the freedom that being single brings and don't let loneliness define your life.

Without a shoulder to lean on and a person to share all these difficult moments, your heart will be filled with sorrow and sadness, and you might not be able to focus on parenthood. You must keep your emotions in check if you want to make it through this turbulent time so that you can safeguard the children from any detriment.

The children will also feel the void left by their other parent, so you have to do your best to keep them occupied, especially if they're still young. This means making sure they have their daily dose of fun and laughter, and in turn, you do too! Also, ensuring that there are people around them, and you, who can provide the attention that you all need.

<u>Parental burnout</u>

This is something that happens to a lot of parents who are single. It's a state of mind brought about by being in your new role as one who is fully responsible for the well-being of your children. It can be caused by the exhaustion that comes with trying to balance work and parenting, especially if you're not getting enough rest and stimulation. Your brain will be overloaded with everything you need to do, so it's essential that you take care of yourself, make sure you get enough sleep, eat healthily and exercise regularly.

Previously, you had someone to assist you with disciplining your children and the household chores, but now that you're a single parent, you have to do it all yourself. You might find it overwhelming at first, but you'll get used to it. Keep reminding yourself of the objective to keep your children happy and healthy, and make sure they don't miss out on anything they need.

If you have spare resources, you may consider hiring a cleaner or childminder to take over some of the responsibilities that come with being a single parent. This way, you'll be able to spend more quality time with the children instead of staying up late trying to finish up the household chores.

Instilling discipline in your children

Children can be sweet and forgiving, but it's also very important to raise them with a strong and firm set of boundaries. You need to teach them good manners and what they can and cannot do. Their safety is in your hands as their guardian, so you have to make sure you're as strict as needed when it comes to discipline.

You should have a firm hand when it comes to instilling discipline in your children, especially if they're young.

Simple acts of disrespect such as talking back, kicking your seat in the car, or even not listening to you may seem like nothing big but can go a long way in ruining their relationship with you as they get older. You need to ensure your children understand that their actions will have consequences. Nip these indiscretions in the bud now so that they don't develop into bad habits that will be hard to break later.

Without a partner to back you up, you have more reason to make certain your children know that you are in charge. You might not feel like the boss of the family, but there's no better time for you to step up and be the parent they need, firm but fair.

It's also vital that you try your best not to show your weaknesses to your children because they may take advantage of them.

There will be times when you'll be required to make the final call on everything from their extracurricular activities to their clothing choices and friends. This can be a difficult mindset to get used to, especially if you're not the type who likes being in charge. But you have to make sure you assert your authority in a kind and compassionate manner to keep them in check.

<u>You may not always know what is "right."</u>

Should you let your child watch TV? Should you cut down on their screen time?

Does your son need to take karate classes, or is it okay for him to do hip-hop dance instead? Should you allow your daughter to pierce her ears and cut her hair short?

These are just some of the many issues that parents, in general, would have to deal with. But as a single parent, you have an even more challenging time because the other parent may not be as vested in the outcomes of these issues. Even if they are supportive of your decisions, it could be very difficult to have to make these kinds of tough calls without their input.

But you can't afford to be indecisive, and you have to make decisions for your child in line with their age and interests.

When your children can tell you how they feel about something, and you cultivate an environment for open and honest dialogue, it'll be easier for you to collaboratively decide on what's best for them.

Overcoming the fear of saying "no"

In as much as you want to say "yes" to your children all the time, you have to be firm about the fact that you are the parent, and there are times when you'll need to say "no."

Assertiveness and self-discipline don't come naturally for a lot of parents, but it's necessary for single parents to learn how to stand up for themselves. It's for their own good, and it's one of the qualities that all successful people possess.

You can also do this with your co-parent before you separate into two separate households. Sit down together and discuss what kind of rules and discipline they want to put into practice for the benefit of the children. This way, hopefully, you both can agree to co-parent in a similar fashion.

It can be hard to confront your children when they throw tantrums and beg you for something, but you must be strong and firm. Make them understand that you have a say in the matter.

Being a single parent isn't easy, but at the end of the day, all you can do is push forward and be the best parent you can possibly be.

Adjusting to single parenthood

One of the best ways to adjust to single parenthood is not to compare yourself to other parents but try instead to focus on your own children and your hopes for them.

You can also check out parenting forums and groups. There are lots of support groups online that you can join and learn from.

There will always be moments when you'll feel like giving up because it's just too crazy, too difficult and way over your head. But don't give up. As a single parent, you need to dig deep and be strong for your children.

In the early days of separation, you'll probably feel a lot of emotions like anger, sadness, and regret, and you're going to want to take out your frustrations on someone. It may be another person, your children, or it may be yourself; you can't let those emotions get the better of you.

Talk about what happened with someone close to you, a friend or family member that you trust can help you through these difficult times. A counsellor or therapist will also be able to help if you're not sure where to start.

If you're emotionally distanced and not able to talk with others, then write down your feelings and get it all out, so you don't have to keep it bottled up inside. You'll feel better when everything is out in the open, and you can start healing.

To be more productive without your co-parent, try changing some of your not-so-good habits; this could mean trying a healthier diet, going on a detox or doing some exercise. Just remember that the best way to work through problems is by seeking solutions.

Look for different ways of handling every situation or problem that arises. Sometimes it's best to be more direct, and other times you might have to be more subtle in your approach. Always ask for help and talk. Know that you are not alone; there are millions of single parents facing similar challenges.

Adjusting to the "I" frame of mind

After the divorce, you won't have access to someone to vent your feelings, like, what a bad day you had at work or how stressful your day was. Neither will you have someone to consult with when you have to make a major decision. You will be on your own and have to learn to adjust to the "I" frame of mind.

A frame of mind refers to the habits, perceptions and thoughts you have. When you were in a relationship, there were certain things that were influenced by your partner, and you don't know or realise it because, naturally, they became a part of you. For instance, you may have stopped watching a favourite TV programme because your partner found it to be irritating. You may also have started to like a certain food that your partner loved.

You knew that if you got in late from work, someone home would wait for you, and if you were tired, there was someone who would help you relax. Now all this and other things that were naturally a part of you are gone, so how will this affect your life?

In the "I" frame of mind, you will have to adjust to the fact that there is no one around who will care for you, who will understand if you are stressed and when the going gets tough, it's all on you.

Prepare yourself mentally to create a working environment where you are your own boss, and you are your own strength. At this stage, you will have to find coping mechanisms to deal with the stress in such a way that it doesn't ruin the rest of your life. You'll feel more alone than ever before because there's no one around to lean on. However, know this: If you do the inner work and learn and grow from this experience - on your own is where you will gain the greatest strength and freedom to create a better life for yourself and your children.

Watching out for stumbling blocks

As you're healing after a divorce, you are experiencing one of the most traumatic times in your life. Having to grieve over lost hopes and dreams, while also striving to keep a positive attitude and move forward with your life is a very hard thing to do. There will be days when you just don't feel like doing anything, and there will be some days where you'll feel like the most amazing person in the world. And when you look at it that way, maybe it isn't as hard as people make out.

After all, if everyone could just accept things the way they are and get on with their lives, life would be great, right? Right! But sadly, that's not how life works. How long do you think it will take for the negative thoughts that are roaming through your mind to start taking a toll on your health? There's no straightforward answer.

Here are a few stumbling blocks you must watch out for during the healing process to protect your health:

Wanting to contact your ex

After a divorce, if you are the party that didn't want to separate, you will probably have the urge to contact your ex or get in touch with them at least once in a while. You'll be thinking about what might have been and how things could have been different. But remember that with every day that passes, the reality of what happened becomes clearer and clearer because you're going through it for yourself.

Self-control is the most important practice at the current time. You need to forgive yourself (and your ex-spouse) and tell yourself that it's not your fault and keep telling yourself until you start believing it. If you're serious about putting your life back together, then that means putting the past behind you once and for all. There's no use trying to contact your ex because they are unlikely to be receptive. The only thing you'll accomplish is to bring more pain onto yourself and prolong the healing process. Don't worry about what might have been, or should have been, just think about what could and what will be.

The "no contact unless it's essential" rule should be the most important thing you follow during this period. If you have children and need to communicate with your ex to make arrangements for contact, then do that. Otherwise, if you were in an abusive relationship, consider changing your number and blocking their calls and messages on social media. If they are persistent and you feel harassed, make a complaint to the police.

Blaming yourself for everything

"If I weren't so bad at marriage and relationships, my ex wouldn't have cheated on me", "I should have been more attentive and more likeable", "If only I didn't post so many pictures of myself online"... and so on. We tend to blame ourselves for everything. We start thinking that there is something wrong with us, or we are just not good enough, and the responsibility rests with us.

If those are the thoughts running through your mind, this is not serving you and will be detrimental to your emotional and psychological well-being. You need to get those thoughts out of your head. You cannot think that way because it is not true. This period of your life is for you to practice self-care and promote self-worth.

Failing to forgive ourselves

We are only human, and we don't always know what is best for us. We tend to second-guess ourselves and wonder why we did certain things.

We need to forgive ourselves for all the mistakes we've made. It's okay if you weren't happy in your marriage and if you ended up having an affair. You can't turn back time, don't dwell on the past. The only thing that matters is what you do now and how you deal with the shortcomings you may have identified. How can we learn and grow from our mistakes and flaws?

It can be hard to forgive yourself for what you did in the past, but it will help you heal faster. Remember that everyone makes mistakes, and nobody is perfect. Handle this situation as well as you possibly can because there will be many more challenges in life. Treat yourself with kindness and compassion like you would treat others in a similar situation.

CHAPTER 12:

FINANCES

The financial side of divorce covers much more than legal costs, and who gets to keep what and who gets to remain in occupation of the family home. It's much deeper than your share of the financial assets. There will be a lot of emotional attachments. It also involves care arrangements for the children, which will impact on the income and capital needs of each party. This chapter will cover all of this and more.

<u>Ending a shared financial life and "the section 25 factors"</u>

While married, you may have shared financial responsibilities. You both took turns paying the bills and filing taxes, and you probably had joint bank accounts. Or it may be the case that you or your ex-spouse took full financial control of all the household finances and investments.

There's also a chance that you had acquired a number of assets before or during the marriage, some jointly owned and others individual. When the marriage comes to an end under English law, you are obligated to make full and frank financial disclosure with a view to dividing matrimonial assets to achieve a fair outcome dependant on the financial positions of each party and their needs.

In chapter 5, Litigation as a last resort, under the sub-heading 'Preparing for litigation', I set out the list of documents and information that you will need to collate for the purposes of preparing your financial disclosure that is undertaken by completing a Form E, if indeed you wish to secure such financial disclosure. This will be required and mandatory if litigating, as the judge will need this information to determine the division of the assets and financial claims.

Some separating couples are happy to agree on financial terms without following this process, as there has been transparency regarding finances throughout their marriage. They trust each other, and they want to save time, money and energy on this process. If so, that is their prerogative, but lawyers (if instructed) will ask for a 'disclaimer' to be signed before they prepare any legal documents to make the terms binding. This is required to cover them from any future lawsuits if you realise at a later stage that you had sold yourself short and settled for less than you were entitled to or there were undisclosed matrimonial assets that you should have had a share of. So, you take your own risks with that option.

If disclosing, you will need to take an inventory of all your assets and liabilities. Assets refer to anything of value you have. Examples are the family home, cars, bank accounts and other savings and investments, including the value of your business interests and pensions. Liabilities are debts or money owed to others. Examples are credit card bills and loan repayments.

There may be justification to *'ring fence'* certain assets as *'non-matrimonial'* to exclude them from the financial assets available for division; the details of the legal position on this are outside the scope of this book, but on such complex issues, it will be wise to seek legal advice.

The starting position will be an equal share of all matrimonial assets. When considering a "fair" division of assets, it is worth keeping in mind the law applicable and the factors a judge will consider when determining a case. A judge may adjust the starting position of an equal split of the assets in either party's favour to ensure there is a fair outcome by reference to the following factors in section 25, Matrimonial Causes Act, 1973, known as "the section 25 factors":

- The income, earning capacity, property, and financial resources each party has or is likely to have in the future. This includes, in the case of earning capacity, any increase in that capacity which it would, in the opinion of the court, be reasonable to expect a party to the marriage to take steps to acquire.

- The financial needs, obligations and responsibilities which each of the parties to the marriage has or is likely to have in the foreseeable future.

- The standard of living enjoyed by the parties before the family breakdown.

- The ages of the parties and duration of the marriage.

- Any physical or mental disabilities that the parties may have.

- The contributions that each of the parties has made or is likely in the foreseeable future to make to the welfare of the family, including any contribution by looking after the home or caring for the family.

- The conduct of the parties where it would be unfair to disregard it.

- The value of a benefit which will be lost by reason of the divorce or nullity of marriage, typically pension rights.

In cases where there are dependent children, the court's first consideration will always be their welfare and how their housing needs will be met.

Caution: It is always wise to consult with a family lawyer and financial planner before you start brokering your own financial terms, so you are clear on your respective rights and responsibilities, as well as any tax implications on any proposals made and agreed upon. If you do not have the financial capacity to secure legal advice, you can access exceptional legal information on these topics via the website 'Advicenow' – it provides clear, step-by-step, user-friendly practical guides to help you manage these types of legal problems.

What about the liabilities? How should these be considered and decided?

This depends on how the debt was incurred and who is responsible for paying the debt. If you have liabilities that are joint or in the sole name of one party and acquired during your marriage with an agreement, then these debts will be classed as 'matrimonial debts', with the starting position being that both parties should take equal responsibility for repayment. But if there is debt that only one party incurred without the consent or knowledge of the other party, then this should be the sole responsibility of the party in whose name it was incurred.

There are times when the court will allocate joint debts to one party. Each case is considered on individual facts and circumstances. So again, it's important that you consult with a family lawyer if you want to know how the court will go about resolving these issues.

How to deal with the matrimonial home

To you, that house where the children grew up is home. It's where memories were made, where family and friends gathered for holidays, and where you spent some of the best times of your life. It also signifies stability, safety and security. To the court, the matrimonial home is just another asset. Just like any other asset, it's subject to division.

When the court considers how to deal with the family home, the primary consideration will be the welfare of any minors to meet their housing needs. In many cases, this can mean that most, or all, of your assets, will go towards providing a home for your children. The priority is to make sure that if one parent has primary care of the children, they have somewhere to live that is suitable for them and the children. It is also important to consider the other parent's need for housing, as well as their need to have somewhere for the children to visit and stay, but the priority will always be meeting the children's housing needs.

You should consider all your options and implications based on your individual financial circumstances and affordability. Is the family home surplus to your needs? Can you afford the upkeep on your own with whatever maintenance you may be entitled to from your ex-spouse? Is it better to have a fresh start, and should the home be sold with the net proceeds divided on a fair basis to help meet the cost of both your housing needs moving forwards? Is there the option for one party to buy the other out? If there is a joint mortgage, will the lender consent to a transfer of the mortgage, or can you secure a new mortgage in your sole name to take over the existing mortgage?

It's worth noting that regardless of whose name the home is in, upon marriage, the starting position is that it becomes a joint matrimonial asset available for division on divorce.

The court is unlikely to order the sale of the family home if it is satisfied that it is affordable and necessary to meet the housing needs of any dependent children. In many cases, there will be an order for a 'deferred trust for sale', which means that the non-occupying spouse will have to wait for his or her share of the equity until specified events occur. Typically, these events are the occupying spouse remarrying or cohabiting with a new partner for a period of 6 months or more, the children reaching 18 years or finishing their full-time secondary education, whichever is the later or the death of the occupying spouse.

Again, it is worth taking legal advice on your rights and options before you reach an agreement on the family home, so you are clear on your rights and what is feasible.

Understanding your new financial needs and obligations

Above, we explored how you will need to sort out assets and liabilities upon divorce, but the other key aspect to consider is sorting out rights to maintenance arising out of your divorce.

This is twofold:

1) Child maintenance for the benefit of any dependent children to meet their upbringing costs.
2) Spousal maintenance to meet your reasonable income needs and living costs.

Depending on the childcare arrangements, be prepared for changes to your financial needs and obligations. If you are the main carer, then there will be extra expenses to meet the children's living costs and needs.

The other parent will have a legal obligation to provide child maintenance in line with the Child Maintenance Service guidelines to support their upkeep. In chapter 8, The child arrangements that need to be made, under the subheading 'Child maintenance support', we set out in more detail how to go about agreeing on child maintenance or invoking the help of the CMS to enforce your rights to child maintenance.

If there is a shared care arrangement in place for the children, each parent will be solely responsible for the children's upkeep while in their care. Often any large expenditure items for the benefit of the children, like the cost of school trips or laptops, will be shared.

If you and your ex-spouse have an equal earning capacity, there will be no entitlement to spousal maintenance. On the other hand, if one party is the higher earner or "the breadwinner" and the other party is "the homemaker" or earns far less, there will be rights to spousal maintenance to support the financially weaker party in meeting their reasonable income needs.

There is no formulaic approach to calculating spousal maintenance. This needs to be assessed by ascertaining each party's net monthly income and comparing this to their monthly income budgets (which should be prepared meticulously). The financially weaker party will require a monthly payment from the financially stronger party to meet their genuine income needs where there is a shortfall between their net income (from all sources) and income needs budget. Failing an agreement, a claim for spousal maintenance may need to be made via a court application for a judge to determine this issue.

Spousal maintenance can be awarded for a specific term (with an opportunity to extend the term before it expires or there may be a bar on any extension request) or on a 'joint lives' basis depending on the specific facts and circumstances of your case. Ideally, divorcing couples should strive for a 'clean break' as soon as possible so long as there is no undue hardship on the financially weaker party.

<u>Moving on, financially, after a divorce</u>

After the divorce, it's important that you prepare financially. While it can be difficult to think about the future and how much money you'll need to take care of your income needs, including any children in your primary care, it's important that you do so.

In this section, we're going to look at the things you should do financially after a divorce as you prepare to raise your children on your own.

Creating a new household budget

You should have at least some idea of what you were both spending on in the past. This will be your point of reference. Financial responsibility means not spending more than you need to. Planning ahead in advance will save you money when it comes time to pay bills and deal with unexpected expenses.

Budgeting serves three purposes: First, it helps you make wise financial decisions because you have a clearer idea of where your money is going. Second, it helps to save you from spending more than you can afford. Third, it enables you to be prepared for the future and make adjustments based on your spending habits.

The Money Helper or Martin Lewis websites are a great place to start gaining control over finances; they have lots of helpful information, tools, and resources to support you, including easy-to-use budget planner templates.

To effectively create a budget, there are some things that need to be considered:

1) Identify your income and expenses. This will include how much money is made per month, how much needs to go into bills, rent/mortgage payments, food costs, transportation costs (car payment, fuel bills), credit card bills, and any other extra costs (entertainment bills).
2) Identify your current debt. This will include mortgages, student loans/other loans, HP agreements, credit cards, and any other debts you currently hold.

3) Identify your needs now and in the future. This will allow you to determine what is essential for "surviving" and what items are not important.

People often overestimate their income and underestimate their spending habits. Write down everything you spend your money on each month. Once you make a list of your monthly expenditure, this list will serve as your guide to creating a realistic budget. Cross-refer to your current bank account statements to help you with this exercise.

Using your list of monthly expenses and the amount of money you make per month will show what you have left over after paying essential bills and other expenses or what the shortfall is.

After calculating your income and expenses, if there is still money left over at the end of the month, it means that you have some savings available for unexpected bills or for future plans. However, if there isn't enough money at the end of each month to cover all monthly expenses, then you may make a claim for spousal maintenance, subject to your ex-spouse having sufficient disposable income. It's also worth looking at ways of supplementing your income or ways of eliminating unnecessary expenditures.

Get an emergency fund

As we've mentioned before, unexpected expenses can put a dent in your finances. It's important to have an emergency fund so that you can cover such expenses without borrowing money from other sources or draining your savings account (if you have any).

This will be your safety net, so it's important to set aside at least a little money each month. Saving for an emergency fund should be done gradually, as you'll want to avoid going into debt.

How much should you save if you do have the financial capacity to save? According to professionals that work within the financial planning sector, you should try to save three to six months' worth of living expenses in your emergency fund. Saving this amount is a good way to make sure you have enough money on hand in case of an emergency. In the unfortunate event that you're laid off or your job is cut back, you'll be okay for a few months whilst you search for and secure another job.

Start eliminating those debts

There are various approaches to debt management and elimination. It is important to speak with a legitimate debt advisor as soon as possible if you are struggling to keep up with payments and finding it hard to manage. Again, refer to trusted websites like Martin Lewis and Money Matters to seek professional guidance and help for free.

The first consideration will be to communicate with your lenders so that they understand your financial constraints after divorce. They will be very receptive, and from my own experience, they may agree to write off part of the debt so long as you disclose your financial position to them on an open and transparent basis. An affordable payment plan can then be agreed.

You may also wish to consider *'consolidation of debts'* so that you only have one payment to make and manage as opposed to several payments.

Sometimes it's in your best interests to start eliminating the highest-interest debt first. Interest is a big expense that eats into your finances, and it's wise to eliminate that first.

If you have one credit card with an interest rate of 20 % and another with an interest rate of 10 %, you'll save money by paying off the 20 % card first. After that, you can focus on paying off the remaining debt at the lower 10 % rate.

There is another approach known as the '*snowball method*' of debt elimination, which means that you pay off all debts with the smallest balances first. This will give you a psychological boost and may motivate you to keep your momentum going until you're completely out of debt.

It's really up to you how you want to go about it; there are pros and cons with all options. With the snowball method, you'll see smaller debts disappear more quickly. This can give you motivation to continue paying off debts because it's more immediate, rather than seeing larger debts like a car loan or mortgage get paid off over time. Part of eliminating debt is a mental game, as well as math. A sense of accomplishment can help a lot in deciding which debts to pay off first.

As suggested already, it is wise to consult with a debt advisor if you are unable to keep up with all your payments and if everything appears to be spiralling out of control. Don't suffer in silence; there are reputable free, and confidential debt advisory services that can help you change the trajectory of your life, like the ones mentioned above.

Start saving and investing for your child's future

Children are expensive. They require a lot of clothes, food, toys, laptops and even their own mobile phones from a fairly young age these days. One of the most important things you can do to prepare for your child's future is to start investing in them while they're still young if you have the financial capacity to do so.

Investing for your child can give them a great start to adult life, helping them go to university, put a deposit on their first home, or to help them go on that adventure that they've always dreamed of.

Junior ISAs are a good place to start. Even a small amount saved each year can snowball into a nest egg over time. Currently, in the UK, you can invest up to £9,000 tax-free. Of course, there are no guarantees, as investments can fluctuate in value. Once opened by a parent or guardian, anyone can contribute to a Junior ISA, making it even easier to invest in their future.

CHAPTER 13:

GRIEVING A BROKEN RELATIONSHIP

<u>Why broken relationships are so painful</u>

We know that separation may lead to depression, but why is this so? What makes parting from someone we love so hard to bear? Scientists have discovered that the brain is structured in such a way as to experience physical pain when it thinks about a lost loved one. Why?

Relationships are a source of pleasure and happiness - the more intense and passionate, the more intense the pleasure. The closer two people are emotionally and physically in the relationship, the greater their mutual pleasures. Why does pain follow the removal of such pleasures?

A breakup induces activity in the part of our brain that also registers physical pain. This is because emotional and physical pain shares the same neural pathways in the brain. Your brain is signalling to your body that a breakup hurts, and those of us that have experienced a breakup know just how bad it hurts.

A study done in 2010 by the American Physiological Society noted that breakups affect three parts of the brain. The mid-brain, the prefrontal cortex and the insular cortex.

The mid-brain is responsible for our reward and motivation centre. Intrinsic motivation is how we get motivated for activities of personal interest, where we get enjoyment and satisfaction internally, and there is no expectation of an external reward. Extrinsic motivation is how we are pushed to do activities that are not necessarily of interest to us, like going to work to pay the bills and to have spend-power.

When there is a breakup, the mid-brain changes its activity to more extrinsic motivation. It is as if there is no intrinsic motivation to sustain the relationship. Without the rewards of being with the person we loved and cared for; the brain changes its focus to outside rewards. This could create discomfort as if you were missing something you need and want in your life. With our reward and motivation system changed by a breakup, we become more open to accepting other benefits in our life.

The prefrontal cortex is affected by cravings mostly. When there is no attention or willingness to stay in a relationship, the prefrontal cortex changes its overall activity. When we "crave" calling our ex after a breakup, wanting to know if they received our text, wanting them to respond to us, etc., that is the prefrontal cortex craving its reward. The same part of the brain that is stimulated with food, alcohol, drugs and sex.

The insular cortex is deeply implicated in self-awareness. In a relationship, this would be emotional awareness and our sense of who we are. A breakup diminishes emotional awareness, leaving us feeling empty and alone as if being stripped of a part of our identity. The emotional distress of being without this person decreases our emotional awareness. As if you are in a fictional world, and things are not as they should be.

Making healthy choices

Don't we all know that we should eat more leafy vegetables, move our bodies more, and get better sleep? We all know what lifestyle changes we should make, but do any of us actually make the time to work at living a healthier lifestyle?

As a result of the worldwide pandemic in 2020/2021 and the profound experiences that we have all endured, many of us have shifted our priorities to looking after our mental health and well-being. It's all about getting our priorities right to serve us better.

If you're like most people, you want your life to be great. You want to feel strong and vibrant and live fully every day. For most of us, however, our lives don't quite turn out that way. Something always has to give for us to do what we have to do each day; go to work to pay the bills, take care of the family and children, do the grocery shopping, cook, clean, and the list goes on and on.

We lose days, months and years of not focusing on our health and blame our hectic life schedules and work, we blame our relatives and friends for losing time because they have encroached on our space, and we lose sleep (key to a healthy lifestyle) because we can't resist the lure of Netflix and the various social media platforms.

We need to make a change in our lifestyle - we can no longer expect to do what needs doing by default. We need to understand that these things are a priority, and if we truly want our lives to be great and become the 'best versions of ourselves', then it's time for us to change.

What is lifestyle change? Lifestyle change could come in many forms, but the most benefit comes in the form of small, consistent changes each and every day that is not too overwhelming or too painful.

For example, in your morning routine, as you get ready for work or the school run, you could listen to a 5-10 minute empowerment meditation to set you up for greatness the rest of the day!

We're naturally resistant to change. As we grow up, we learn that the world is a complicated, demanding place, one which demands that we stay on top of things all the time. For us to achieve this, we need to make healthy life choices. By healthy choices, we're not just talking about our physical well-being. There is a need to be in a relationship with others and the world around us. Do you remember when we said that we'll take a holistic approach to divorce? One that looks at our physical health, our mental well-being, our emotional state, and our spiritual well-being. Let's start with physical health.

Our physical health

A healthy lifestyle involves making choices that improve our physical health and well-being. The choices we make can have a positive or negative impact on how we feel about ourselves and how our bodies feel. Learning to eat nutritiously, looking for ways to be more physically active and practicing stress-management techniques are just a few of the habits that will help keep your body functioning at its best - this will help you feel good about yourself too.

Losing weight or maintaining a healthy weight will help you look good and feel great, and having regular check-ups with your doctor is another way to ensure that you're not headed down an unhealthy path.

Comfort foods - many foods that seem so delicious may actually be "diabetes heaven" in disguise. The way to avoid this is to eat healthier versions of the comfort food that you love. Sprinkling a bit of cinnamon on apple slices as they bake will make that apple taste even better and give your body what it needs (a sugar hit!) in a healthier way to help keep unhealthy hunger pangs at bay.

Another way that you might improve your physical health is with exercise. If you have a regular exercise routine, it will increase your metabolism and help burn off excess calories, keeping you lean and trim. You can also increase your metabolism by increasing the amount of physical activity in which you engage each day. You can start in small increments and build up to a 5K run with the *'Couch to 5K'* runner APP, (like I did!) to help keep up your stamina. Walking is one of the best forms of exercise outside with Mother Nature; maybe take it a step further and jog.

You don't have to pay for any gyms or gym equipment to get a good workout; the stairs are free! Even if they are a bit tricky at first, this is one of the best cardiovascular exercises ever. Hobbies that have a physical aspect, such as bowling or bike riding, will help you get in shape.

Our mental well-being

Pursue a hobby that you love; doing something you love is a great stress reliever. Many of us spend most of our days and time at work to meet our financial obligations, but finding activities outside work that you enjoy doing is a great way to feel more fulfilled and happier overall. If you like gardening, for example, try growing some vegetables on your patio or balcony.

When we're deeply involved in a hobby or passion, we often forget to be self-critical and aware of our outward appearance. Enthusiasm for your hobbies and passions will help you feel good and look great as well!

Taking a break to unwind is also a great way to reduce your stress levels and maintain your mental well-being. For example, if you like listening to songs and music, blast your favourite tunes to take a break for no other reason than you love it, and it brings you joy! Downtime can be free time that you spend relaxing with friends or family members, or even alone, reading a book or doing some light yoga.

I follow 'Yoga With Adriene' and have done so for the past several years. She has been a Godsend in my healing journey. THANK YOU, Adriene. Her YouTube channel provides high-quality practices on yoga, meditation and mindfulness at no cost to inspire people across the globe of all ages, shapes and sizes to take this wonderful practice up. I highly recommend it. Check her out; you've got nothing to lose and everything to gain!

Make daily phone calls to friends and family. After the divorce, you may have become quite isolated from the world and your family and friends. Taking time to reconnect and call your friends and family on a regular basis will reassure them that you are doing well. They can help you get through your divorce by providing support, laughter, and some great conversation. My family, my "inner circle", were very supportive during these times. I don't think I would have come through it without their care and attention. THANK YOU, mum, dad, Shan, Mish, Resh, Nik and Kaj.

Solitude is good for our mental health. Whether you're taking a long walk; sitting on a bench at a nearby park; or sitting on your patio contemplating life, being alone can help you clear your mind. It gives you time to think about everything that's been happening in your life, and it allows you to come up with solutions to any problems that may be keeping you from moving forward and feeling positive about your future.

Our emotional state

After the divorce, our emotions may be all over the place. That's normal. It's important to learn how to control and regulate negative emotions, such as anger or sadness, in order to maintain a more even keel during those difficult times of healing through the divorce process.

It's also important to learn how to express your emotions in a healthy way. Talking about what's happening to you with friends or family can help you feel better and more in control of your life. Finding a safe place where you can share concerns, fears, and frustrations will help ensure that you don't let those emotions get the better of you. It's worth considering working with a divorce coach or therapist to help you with this and get your life back on track

You can also use healthy outlets for anger and frustration. Some safe ways include taking a long brisk walk or hike, taking up boxing or an interactive sport, or listening to music that makes you want to dance or work out until you've burned off whatever negative feelings are caused by the divorce.

Identifying emotions such as 'sadness' or 'disappointment' is the first step to learning how to handle them. You can also take time each week to focus on your feelings so that, at some point, you'll have worked through your emotions and won't feel so miserable.

Watching the news might irritate you and keep you up at night. Especially with all that is going on in the world currently and over the past few years. Watching the news constantly can cause physical changes inside the body, such as elevated heart rate, blood pressure and digestive issues. The stress of listening to the news can also have a negative impact on our emotional state.

Some people may benefit from a complete detox from the news for a period of time. Or maybe switch to watching the news only once a day, earlier in the day as opposed to night-time. I'd suggest keeping the intake brief to the headlines only. That way, you will have an overview of what's happening in your community and the world at large, but you won't feel overwhelmed and stressed from watching it.

Our Spiritual well-being

By spirituality, we're referring to being connected to something bigger than ourselves. A belief in higher consciousness and intelligence that runs the universe both in life and after death. Some people understand this concept as 'God', and for others, there is no God; it's about a belief in their 'Higher Selves'.

There are many definitions of spirituality; some are religious, and others are without any religious connotations. For me, it is the latter. I have a strong belief that we are all connected and are one, regardless of our race, colour, creed, gender, sexual orientation etc. I believe that we are more than just our physical bodies and minds and that our true essence, spirit, and energetic body are eternal and never die.

Many forms of spirituality can be beneficial, from finding a spiritual group to join to get a sense of community, to attending a church for regular Sunday service. Or you may consider taking up an interest in the arts, such as painting or performing arts, like dance or amateur acting, to help you improve your mental and physical well-being.

If you're feeling low in spirit and not sure how you will ever overcome the stress and pain that is a part of divorce, consider working towards attaining higher levels of spirituality by going on retreats with other people who are interested in improving their lives as well. If you are curious about spiritual retreats, you've got to lean in and find out more through your own enquiries online and take a leap of faith in anything that sparks your interest to experience it for yourself. Again, you've got nothing to lose and everything to gain!

Doing good deeds can be a great way to help those around you. Doing charitable work is a perfect way to relieve stress and improve your mental health and well-being. This also keeps you connected to a higher purpose beyond yourself. For example, you can donate blood; buy food for the homeless; or volunteer at a soup kitchen.

Spiritual pursuits are also beneficial for our emotional well-being. Whatever your spiritual path happens to be, learning about it and finding ways to incorporate that into your daily life can help you maintain balance in your quest to heal from the divorce process.

There are overlaps between all these practices, and many people will use more than one of them at a time. Again, the important thing is to try to find activities that help you feel more alive and connected to the world around you.

That could be through taking a long walk, practicing yoga, or going on a weekend trip with your friends. Eventually, after enough time, you will find that you have improved your emotional stability and can feel more positive about your outlook and life again.

Reclaiming your life

If I was to describe what starting afresh feels like, I would say that it feels like being born again. It's a rebirth. You can't go back in time, but you can move forward to a place where life is once again full of hope, faith and happiness.

You experience relief knowing that the divorce process is over, and now you can move on to your future. Not worrying about how it will all turn out helps reduce stress and anxiety. Trust the process and know that whatever happens, happens for the best.

Moving forward means reclaiming your life by integrating new activities into your daily life, reconnecting with old friends and making new friends, and learning some new hobbies so that you have more things to do than just sitting around brooding or thinking about the past. It also means being kinder to yourself and accepting the fact that time has passed, and you need to move on with your life.

Controlling your emotional state can be difficult at first, but remember that with practice, you will reach a point where you feel stronger than before and ready for whatever lies ahead. Be sure to practice accepting whatever happens in your future.

In his books, Dr Seuss tells children, "Don't cry because it's over; smile because it happened." Learning to do that is a very difficult thing for most people, and it takes time. But the reward is well worth the time and effort you put into learning how to move on with your life after a divorce.

It may take some hard work to improve your emotional state, but it's worth it in the end because you will feel happier, healthier and ready for whatever comes next.

Taking personal responsibility

You're the only one who can change the future. When we blame our ex, the children, the court, the weather, the culture or whichever culprit we can think of, we're giving them power over our lives. Blame steals two things from us. It robs us of our agency and self-confidence, and it creates an overwhelming sense of shame.

The reality is that things just don't always turn out the way you want them to. You can't control the actions of others, so blaming and shaming yourself or others for things beyond your control will only make you feel worse about yourself.

As you work to improve your emotional state by learning how to manage and regulate your emotions and take care of yourself, try not to be self-critical about how much time it's taking for you to heal.

How can we learn to take responsibility for our well-being?

It starts with acknowledging that we're in control

The universe may throw us curve balls, but ultimately, it's up to us how we respond to those curve balls. We should be in control of our own actions, and there are no excuses for our behaviour.

Taking personal responsibility after divorce comes from accepting that it was our actions (or the lack thereof) that got us here in the first place. Feelings can come and go, but you can make yourself feel better about your situation by taking action. Taking action can be as simple as deciding to watch a funny movie with a friend instead of watching the evening news or reading an inspirational book instead of one that makes you feel bad about your life.

By taking responsibility for your life, you are acknowledging that you do have the power to improve your circumstances and future trajectory.

You are ready to start living your life again and want to put the past behind you. This is a very difficult thing to do, but personal responsibility is one of the tools that can help you create a productive lifestyle after divorce.

Taking the first steps on this path will be challenging because it means admitting that we've made mistakes in our lives that led us here, and now we need to fix them. After the separation, there may be so much to do, but you are more determined than ever now to move on with your life.

Remember that feelings will come and go, and they won't take away the fact that you made mistakes. Take responsibility for your own actions because it is important to learn how to handle our emotions in a positive way so that we can get through the divorce process.

You can start by learning from the past and improving your future.

Realise that you have power over your emotions

Remorse, regret, guilt, shame and grief can be powerful emotions that can consume you. After breaking up with your ex, you may feel a serious sense of regret and shame, but those feelings will go away.

It is important to remember that your emotions can not last forever, so don't give in to these negative emotions by spending all day being miserable. Start doing something positive with your time to change your mood, frequency and emotions.

Start living for today

You can start making positive changes in your life today by becoming more aware of how you are feeling. The first thing you need to do is learn to calm down and how to regulate the emotions that you're feeling, such as anger or anxiety. It will help tremendously if you remind yourself that these feelings are normal for anyone going through a breakup or divorce.

Unpacking your baggage

"Relationship baggage" is a term that refers to the emotional stress that comes from all the things you've done in previous relationships. You may have learnt specific behaviours in your past (such as blaming, fighting, talking behind each other's backs or being insecure) that may come back to haunt you in your present situation.

These can be dangerous because they make us feel vulnerable, angry and frustrated. As part of the healing process after divorce, we'll get rid of the scars that we may have accumulated throughout the years.

This is a very healthy way to let go of the past. The first step is to identify the negative feelings and recognise them as normal emotions that everyone experiences when they go through a breakup.

Don't be afraid of your own feelings; in fact, embrace them so you can start working through them with a new outlook and positive point of view. Work towards resolving all the negative emotions that are making you feel down by doing something positive each day.

Betrayal, loss, anger and sadness are common emotions that you'll feel after a divorce. Negative feelings happen to everyone, but they will fade in time. It's important to acknowledge those feelings and work through them during the healing process.

You don't have to force yourself to feel happy when you are sad; instead of trying to run away from your emotions, learn how to embrace and 'feel' them and find a way to release them so you can move on with your life after a divorce. Having an emotional breakdown, letting go of the pain and emotions by crying, screaming, shouting and doing whatever it takes in a safe and supported environment is necessary for you to heal.

These negative emotions will affect your actions and cause you to act in ways that may not be in your best interest. You may try to avoid the situation or ignore it, but it will only make you feel worse. The longer you wait, the worse it will become.

Instead of trying to avoid facing your emotions, take action by finding a way to resolve these feelings so they don't continue to block your path towards happiness. The first step is to write down any negative feelings on paper. Then, imagine that those thoughts and feelings are tied to a halogen balloon that goes up with them into the sky once released. Gone forever. Or maybe the symbolic act of tearing up the paper or safely burning it can have a huge positive impact on your emotional and psychological well-being.

<u>Finding closure to the pain of divorce</u>

We've seen that the "baggage" we may be holding on to from previous relationships will hurt us mentally and emotionally. We may feel completely stuck because we're not willing to let go of the past.

When we don't accept that we are in control of our own actions and destiny, it means that we are holding on to blame and resentment towards our ex. This can be very discouraging. Recognise that it's time to move forward with your life after divorce.

We must learn how to find closure with the situation to move forward and put the past behind us so we can start living again. If we let these negative feelings build up inside of us, we'll eventually explode, destroying everything around us.

To do this, we first need to identify those "what ifs" that pop up in our heads, especially the ones related to our ex.

Thoughts like:

- What if I hadn't married them?
- What if I could have done it differently?
- What if they had never said or done that?
- What if I had taken note of all the warning signs?
- What if I had been a better wife/husband?

When these thoughts come into your mind, remind yourself that you can't change the past. You can't go back to the day when you met your ex, and you can't undo what happened. Accept that things happened the way they did for a reason, and it's now time to move on with your life. Acceptance and letting go are the two sure ways to set yourself free.

When you hold on to these negative thoughts, it's normal to feel anger towards our ex or regret about what we should've done differently. But that is not going to change anything; in fact, it will only make us feel worse and make us focus even more on the past. It will be healthier and easier, if we let things go and move forward with our lives after divorce. Don't waste your precious time and energy on "what should have been, what would have been, and what could have been."

CHAPTER 14:

A SUPPORT SYSTEM

The loneliness and confusion that accompanies divorce can feel like it's insurmountable at times. When we're faced with challenges in life, we often seek advice from our friends, but talking about our marital problems can be difficult and embarrassing. It could be because we're experiencing major changes in our life where we prefer being alone or simply because we don't want to burden our friends with our problems. The fear of being judged by our friends could also hold us back, but this is a mistake because we should be upfront and honest with them.

Don't be afraid to express your feelings openly because everyone needs a shoulder to lean on whenever they're feeling down or broken. You may want to talk to a therapist, counsellor or divorce coach if you don't feel comfortable with your family or friends. They can help you get out of this difficult situation and move forward in your life without hiding your pain or secrets.

Getting help from a support system is key to keeping your head above water and not drowning when going through a divorce. In this chapter, we're going to look at what you can do to get the support that you need from loved ones on your journey after divorce, but before we get to that, let us make one thing clear, it's okay to ask for help.

It's OK to ask for help

We're social creatures that find solace and comfort in other people. At times like this, however, we can feel lonely in a crowded room.

We bond easily with other people, and when we see someone around us in pain or going through something difficult, it's natural for us to want to help that person out, whether it's by offering our shoulder to cry on or simply lending a listening ear. Those that can relate to a situation or have gone through it themselves can be a great source of comfort to us.

As you're going through a divorce, you'll feel isolated and vulnerable. Sharing what's going on with close family or friends will help you feel less alone and give you the support you need to get through it and move on with life. There are also divorce support groups that you can join to talk about how you are feeling and to help you accept the end of your marriage

The benefits of a support system

The most obvious benefit of joining a support group is that it will make you feel less alone. No matter how tough or strong you are, divorce is still a difficult time for everyone, especially if you're caught off guard by the news. It's not easy to accept that your marriage is over, and it's even harder to accept that you need to co-parent with your ex.

These are the other benefits of joining a support group:

You get to vent your anger and frustrations about what is happening in your life without being judged by others or being told what to do next.

Sometimes we're looking for someone to advise us. At other times, we need someone to hear us. Talking it out is a coping technique that a lot of people use in times like these. The best way to deal with our emotions is by expressing them through conversation.

When we don't choose to talk about what is going on for us, the frustration and pain that we're feeling will build up inside of us, eventually exploding in a show of anger. So, it's important to have someone around you that you can trust and open up to.

You'll be given useful tips during your journey through divorce

We just got out of a relationship where we were used to certain things. In fact, when we get married, we accept our partners as they are and learn how to live with them. When the marriage ends, we get used to living alone again, and it's not always easy adjusting back to our original single lifestyle, but you will. Those who have been through similar situations can give you a new perspective and help you understand that what you're going through is temporary.

It's a way of letting go

When things don't work out in a relationship, there is a lot of resentment that builds up inside us. It's human nature to be upset when things don't go the way we had planned, and it only escalates with time. The best way to get over the bitterness and hostility towards your ex-spouse is by letting things go. We're taught from an early age that if we have hurt someone badly, we should apologise and ask for forgiveness.

Hiding negative feelings from other people isn't healthy; this is why coming out of the shadows will enable you to let go of those unnecessary negative emotions that have been weighing you down.

It puts a perspective on life

Divorce isn't the worst thing that can happen to a person. While it may seem terrible right now, we'll eventually learn to accept the changes in our lives and move on. While being supportive of us, someone who went through a similar situation can give us great perspective and help us realise that we aren't alone in our current predicament.

When we're in a relationship that ends up failing, it's easy to go down the "blame game", blaming our ex and ourselves for what went wrong. We may be going through self-loathing and other negative emotions because we think that something is not right with us. Instead of looking at the marriage as a failure, look at it as an opportunity for you to better understand yourself and your ex-spouse, and realise why things didn't work out between you two.

It could be a way to make new friends

If you choose to join a divorce support group or forum (there are plenty to choose from on the various social media platforms), there is a good chance that you'll meet new friends. You may have lost one-half of your relationship, but at least you found the perfect companion to help you cope with the situation and let you get back on your feet. Those who are going through a similar experience will be able to understand what you're going through and give advice and encouragement as well.

By hearing the experiences of others and meeting people with similar circumstances, you will be able to recognise that there are people out there who are going through the same challenges as you. You just have to find a divorce support group that resonates with you and make yourself available.

<u>Reaching out to friends and family</u>

When we're struggling to cope with reality, how do we initiate a conversation with those we care a lot about, like our closest friends and family? We're afraid that they'll be upset with us and maybe judge us for the marriage breakup. We could also fear that we'll be left vulnerable after exposing our weaknesses to them. How do we go about talking to them?

The best way to initiate the conversation if you are struggling to call them is through messaging. Initiate the conversation with a simple "Hi." After exchanging pleasantries, we could make the transition to a deeper conversation by first asking your friend or family member to share any highs and lows they've had recently.

You could word it this way, "It's been a few days since we caught up. How are you? Maybe we could use a few minutes to share the highlights and lowlights of our own lives."

After that, you could share your own experience and how you're coping with the situation. You could start off with, "It's been a year since our divorce. I'm so lost right now because I don't know where my life is heading. I feel like I can't trust anyone anymore."

It's up to you how you want the conversation to go and what you want to share, but don't put them on the spot and expect them to have all the answers. Also, it's important to remember that you can't control their response. Some people may be abrupt in their response and tell you what they think of your situation. Others may be more kind and patient and give you some advice and support. The best mindset is to not feel offended by their reaction; they're just being themselves and doing the best they can to support you in the only way they know how.

<u>Seeking help from a therapist or divorce coach</u>

Family therapists and divorce coaches have assumed a central position in society's response to the contemporary family breakup crisis. From providing support for couples facing the risk of separation and divorce through to helping parents repair their damaged relationships after divorce, family therapists and coaches today are dedicated to helping separating and divorcing couples process and deal with their emotions and difficulties. On many occasions, they support them to effect a reconciliation if this is what is desired.

Talking to a therapist or coach may be better than reaching out to friends and family because you'll get a more objective view of what's been causing you to be unhappy and the steps you can take to improve the situation. They're trained to be unbiased and approach the situation with an open mind. Many are also trained in conflict resolution and anger management; they're able to help you identify your problems and discuss solutions to the problems in a safe, confidential and non-judgemental environment.

'Cognitive behavioural therapy' known as 'CBT' is one of the key techniques used by coaches and family therapists today to treat countless of individuals and couples looking to overcome their difficulties. It's not tied to any religious or political institution and is more focused on immediate results; this means that you'll get relief from your symptoms in no time at all. CBT is a talking therapy that can help you manage your problems and emotions by changing the way you think and behave.

It's most commonly used to treat anxiety and depression but can be useful for other mental and physical health problems too. The technique is grounded in the belief that how a person perceives events (their thoughts) determines how they will act. It is not the events themselves that determine the person's actions or feelings.

CHAPTER 15:

SELF CARE

Divorce is a journey from "we" to "me." But it's a journey few of us look forward to taking. As your divorce approaches (or begins), you may wonder if there's any way to preserve your sanity and a reasonable level of happiness along the way, even as you cope with having your life turned upside down. The good news is that, yes, there are things you can do to help ease the pain and discomfort of divorce while building yourself up and strengthening your support system.

Self-care is exactly like it sounds. It is to nurture yourself and your family, especially when you are going through a major life transition such as divorce. It can be hard to pull yourself out of the "rut" of divorce-related stress when it's all around you. Sometimes, it just feels impossible. This chapter will help you. Join me as we explore ways you can practice self-care while going through a divorce.

What is self-care?

Simply put, self-care is the practice of taking care of yourself and your emotional and mental needs. It's not easy, but in the long run, it has lots of benefits. While going through a divorce, self-care is all about maintaining sanity and a good state of mind whenever you can.

Self-care is about doing the things that make you feel simultaneously relaxed and invigorated. You feel like you are still in control, not your ex-spouse or anyone else in your life. It is about making yourself a priority and taking care of yourself physically, mentally, emotionally and spiritually.

A positive mindset

A positive mindset is vital and key to a happy future and a good self-care routine. If you're not looking for the silver lining, you won't see it. If you keep telling yourself that life will never be the same, it won't. But if you remind yourself that you can still do and be what you want, you will. This is known as the '*self-fulfilling prophecy*'.

A positive mindset is one that is full of hope and optimism about the future instead of dread and sadness about your current situation.

It requires you to hold on to your sense of humour when you feel like letting go. It keeps you from feeling sorry for yourself when things aren't going well. When thinking positively, you're cultivating an attitude that will enable you to break free from being a victim in any way, shape or form.

How can we develop it?

Focusing on the good things in life is one of the ways we can maintain a positive mindset. We've heard it before; it's hard to feel sad when you're focusing on the good things around you.

When you're feeling down, try doing one or more of these things to lift your spirits:

1) Find the humour in your situation.

You don't have to be a stand-up comedian to find humour in everyday situations. When we can laugh with each other and at ourselves, it gets easier to let go of the stress that comes with divorce.

2) Take a deep breath and connect within.

3) Think of something you are grateful for.

A daily practice of gratitude is like a magic tonic that will uplift your spirits to a higher positive frequency.

4) Ask yourself the right questions.

"If you change the way you look at things, the things you look at change."- Dr Wayne Dyer.

5) Tell someone else about your feelings.

6) Ask for help when you need it.

None of us are Superman or Wonder-woman, although we'd like to think we are! Sometimes, we all need some help from others, even if we don't want to admit it. If your friends and family are supportive, ask them to help keep your spirits up during this difficult time.

Our mindset is also affected by the way that we communicate with other people. When you're going through a divorce, you want to be mindful of the way that you express yourself to others, especially your ex-spouse and children.

People say things without thinking sometimes, and those hurtful words can stick in your mind and make it harder to keep a positive mindset and be compassionate.

If you feel like you're about to get into an emotional argument, take time out to calm down before you respond. If you need to, walk away from the conversation so that you can come back when you're able to express yourself constructively.

There are lots of things that can be done to help promote a positive mindset during and after divorce. Surround yourself with positive people who want to see you succeed and be happy in your own life. If they're not going through the same thing, they might not get it at first, so don't be afraid to help them understand what you're going through without being too negative or sad.

Self-talk is how we speak to ourselves inside our own heads (our internal voice). It's very important to have a positive self-talk voice during times of stress and turbulence like divorce.

One way that our self-talk can be negative is if we use phrases such as: "There's no way I can do it", or "This will never work out." Using words like "never" or "can't" when talking to yourself about a situation is a guaranteed way to put yourself into a negative spin and mindset.

Instead, whisper words of encouragement to yourself like: "I can be the person I want to be", or "I am strong and powerful."

Self-talk is an important part of self-care when going through a divorce. If you tell yourself you can do it, you'll believe it! And if you're confident in your ability to succeed, then others will be too. When we take care of ourselves by practicing self-care, we give our bodies and minds the rest that they need.

The subconscious mind picks up on our words, and we start acting in ways that are consistent with the things that we say to ourselves. When you're practicing self-care, you might be saying, "It's okay to take some time out for myself," and you will do just that!

Building the resilience necessary to withstand the emotional hurricane

A tough mental core is the most important ingredient in learning how to endure pain without suffering. We must learn to endure pain without allowing it to define us, beat us down or keep us from getting the most out of life. Resilience is what we develop when we push through our own personal discomfort, exert ourselves and then rest up before pushing even harder.

To get through this difficult time, we will all need to develop our resilience. Developing resilience is a process that requires effort, but it's worth it in the end.

The first step in developing your resilience is to give yourself a break. Allow yourself the time that you need to rest, re-set, renew and reconnect with yourself before getting back into the fray. Although it's easy to give into feeling sorry for yourself and wallow in pity, it's actually much better for your psyche and physical well-being to check out and take some time out. If you feel like you're at the end of your rope, know that there are people who care about you and who have gone through this experience many times already. It is okay to feel miserable.

Avoid making grandiose promises to yourself about how you're going to get better and be happy. The best thing we can do is to promise ourselves that we'll try to do the best we can, in the moment, without obsessing about outcomes.

We will all have our ups and downs during divorce, and it's normal to feel depressed and anxious from time to time. Just remember, there is always hope, and you will survive this, no matter what!

Like everything else, learning how to be resilient and developing a "tough mental core" takes effort and practice. But you'll see that with time; it will become easier.

When we start by squashing our insecurities and fears, we can begin to develop the resilience necessary to withstand the emotional hurricane of divorce.

On those dark days when you feel like you can't do any more, remember:

- You are not alone.
- It's okay to ask for help when you need it.
- You will survive this, no matter what.

By thinking of the other storms that we've stood in our lives, we can remind ourselves that we can survive the current one too and go on to thrive!

To get through any given situation, we need to give ourselves a break and allow ourselves time to rest and recharge. Sometimes, it just takes us time to realise that this is what we need.

Taking care of your mental health while co-parenting

Four things make divorces awful:

1) We're sad that we're no longer together.
2) We worry about our children's well-being because of the turmoil in our current situation.
3) We're not sure if we made the right decision and/or if it was the right time.
4) We all have to co-parent with a former partner who may or may not be on the same page and in sync with us.

The person we're divorcing appears to be the focal point, and we'll still be in touch for the good of the children even after parting ways. It's not easy to use the "out of sight, out of mind" principle - this doesn't work when you share children and a parental role with your ex.

Co-parenting will come with its own challenges, but you can still try searching for a solution that is mutually agreeable.

But remember that you have to prioritise yourself first and be mindful of your mental health at all times.

You will come across situations where emotions will get the better of you and make you wonder if you are doing the right thing. Take a break from your hectic life and do what lifts your spirit.

Take time to write down how you feel so that you can look back later and see how far you have come since your divorce was finalised.

There are things that can help you cope with your feelings, and there are things that will just make you stress out. You have to find a balance.

Here are four things that you can do to take care of your mental health:

1) **Acknowledge and accept it**: Your ex is still a part of your life - and that's not going to change (unless there are extenuating circumstances that calls for a complete severance of ties). You may move on, but he or she is still going to be part of your children's life. In a way, you have to accept that you are still a co-parent, and you will have to talk about the children with your ex. Accepting the situation is the first step.

2) **Separate emotions from the truth**: Be objective about the things you and your ex discuss about the children. Try to be positive in what you say because that's going to have a much better effect on your children rather than just blurting out negative comments.

3) **Speak up if something hurts**: This may be difficult for you, but sometimes, it's best to agree to disagree. Disagreeing does not make you a bad person and can actually help things run smoothly. Politely tell your ex what bothers you so that he or she will understand the boundaries of your relationship with them. Keep all communication civil and never go beyond the boundaries of a polite disagreement.

4) **Don't beat yourself up**: Try not to beat yourself up about things said and done in the past and now between you and your ex. Remember that none of us

are saints, and we all have flaws. Forgive yourself and your ex. Let it go and set yourself free.

Spending time with loved ones

No self-care routine is complete without spending some quality time with your family and loved ones. Doing things you enjoy like watching a movie, planning a trip or going out for dinner, will help you unwind and shift your mind from the negative things that happened in the past.

You don't even need to "do" anything. Having a chat with your mother or watching your daughter play will help you unwind and let you forget the stresses and strains in your life. Whenever you feel like you are drowning in your own problems, take a step back and look at things objectively.

Catch up with close friends and humour how marriage isn't your thing, get on a rollercoaster and scream with strangers, listen to your favourite song or watch a chick flick and have a good cry. Go ahead and feel all the emotions that you should, then start anew.

Take time for yourself and make sure that you continue living your life, despite situations currently not being in your favour. Start treating yourself better and learn to be happy with what you have now rather than thinking about what you had in the past. Focus on taking care of yourself because if you don't, no one else will.

Self-compassion

We're our own worst critics, and during separation and divorce, this can get intensified. We will have a huge amount of self-loath and self-critical talk going on in our minds that blow reality out of proportion. When we tell ourselves stories about our failings and shortcomings, it makes us feel inferior and unworthy. We start believing that the whole world is against us and that we don't deserve to be happy.

The practice of self-compassion is being more understanding, gentle and kinder to yourself. Allowing yourself the grace to grow and learn from these life experiences. It's recognising that we all have a part to play in a relationship and its breakup.

By practicing self-compassion, you will show a tremendous amount of love and self-acceptance and will be able to heal much faster, let go of the past and realise that you deserve happiness in life too.

Mindfulness

Scientists say, on average, our brains process between 50,000 and 70,000 thoughts every day! From when we wake up to when we fall off to sleep, we are constantly processing thoughts from what we'll make for our dinner, if we'll have time to go grocery shopping, did we remember to put out the washing to self-critical thoughts like, "I'm such an idiot, why did I do that?" Our minds are always active, and thoughts come in like waves crashing against the shore.

We couldn't possibly control every thought that we have in a day; that's impossible. We will have thoughts of failure or achieving success, we will think of our boss shouting at us and telling us to do better, or about getting a new job because we're not really happy where we are, we'll think about our ex-spouse and how things were when we were together and what should have, could have been and so on.

How many of these thoughts are motivated by something that is true? How many of these thoughts are a conditioned response towards something that we are told to think? Think back to all the times you had negative thoughts towards someone or something. Were they genuinely true, or did they just come at you because you were conditioned to think that way?

80% of our thoughts are negative, and 95% of our thoughts are repetitive; that's a whole lot of negative repetitive thoughts!

Mindfulness is the practise of watching your thoughts as they come and go and tuning into your body and emotions. As you get better at it, you can quickly become aware of when your mind is wandering in all sorts of different directions and the sensations and emotions you are feeling.

When you are mindful, you take control of your thought process and stop letting your emotions dictate how you feel about yourself. By taking back control of your mind, you can learn to relax and remain calm at times when previously, there was anxiety and panic.

Mindfulness lets us stand back from our thoughts and start to see their patterns. Gradually, we can train ourselves to notice when our thoughts are taking over and realise that our thoughts are often not accurate and that they can be changed.

Mindfulness can help us deal with issues more productively. We can ask: "Is trying to solve this by worrying about it helpful, or am I just getting caught up in my thoughts?"

How mindfulness helps when going through a divorce

When going through a divorce, it seems as if your whole world is falling apart. You are emotionally exhausted due to arguing with your ex-spouse, going to court, having sleepless nights because you're anxious about the future, you're worried about how you'll make enough money for yourself after the divorce and so on.

It's difficult for us to think of happier times rather than focusing on what's happening right now, which is understandable given that negative emotions will always be stronger than positive emotions until we learn to let go. It's not like we can change what happens in the future, but it is possible to go from being negative and unhappy to being positive and happy. Negative thoughts are constantly stimulating the stress hormone cortisol in our bodies which makes us feel terrible, so we won't achieve anything until we let go of the negative thoughts.

Being more mindful will have these benefits:

It's a stress-relief technique

You'll start to notice when negative thoughts come into your mind, and you will be able to change them. This will help you learn how to be happier in life without depending on events that happen. All you have to do is become more aware of your thoughts and realise that they are not always true, so by changing them, you'll become a happier person who is less stressed out.

You'll break the cycle of negative emotions

Once negative thoughts come into your mind, other negative emotions will come right after. It's like a domino effect, and once one thought comes into your mind, it discharges neurotransmitters in your body that causes other thoughts to come in and so on.

By becoming aware of your thoughts, you will be able to stop this domino effect before it happens. Once you let go of the negative thoughts, your emotions will start to change, and other more positive feelings like joy, love and happiness will appear.

It's a stress relief technique that helps you get over your ex-spouse quicker

When we feel sad or depressed because of something that has happened, it can take months or years for us to get over it by ourselves, which is understandable because we might not know how to turn our emotions around. Mindfulness can help us do that much quicker because once we notice negative thoughts in our minds, we can get rid of them immediately by changing our thinking and thought patterns, which reduces stress in the body.

<u>Evaluating areas that need to change</u>

Mindfulness is a troubleshooting tool. By becoming an external observer, a witness to our actions and thoughts, we're able to see the things that we're doing right and those that could be hindering our recovery after a divorce. For instance, we may notice that we're easily angered and let the stress build up for days on end. This will cause tension not only towards our ex-spouse but also our children, if we have any, and other people around us.

It's important to carry out this evaluation because your thoughts might be stressing you out more than you realise. Sometimes, it's hard to know what is causing the stress until you look at all the different areas of your life and see where you're having problems that could be improved. You'll be surprised how many things in your life can be fixed by even just a small change in how you think or act. By actively practicing mindfulness, it can have a huge positive impact on the outcome of what happens next in your life.

Mindfulness can be a useful tool for constructive self-critique. You'll be more aware of how you deal with the things that are affecting your mood. For example, after noticing that you're easily angered by others, you can correct that behaviour and make a conscious effort to become more relaxed by using other tools like breath work and yoga to regulate your emotions.

<u>Healing after a divorce through Yoga</u>

There's something therapeutic about stretching the body in new ways. Could it be that it helps us to move beyond our current life circumstances and to heal our wounds? Can an emotional wound be healed with a physical stretch?

Yoga, the ancient science of stretching from India, has many benefits. In fact, it can be viewed as a workout for the mind, body, spirit and soul because it provides stress relief, relaxation, and strength and connects us to our higher self and consciousness. In simple terms, yoga means union with the Divine.

Yoga helps separating couples heal in a number of ways.

First, it's a way of releasing past trauma as well as worry and tension from present problems. It is a form of meditation where we watch our breath and choose to let go of what's weighing us down. There is a feeling of freedom and ease you can experience in yoga.

Students of Maharishi Patanjali (a great spiritual leader of ancient times known as the "Father of Yoga") believe that performing these poses opens the heart and enables you to become a better person. It is a practice that helps you become more loving, compassionate and joyful, and it can also help you to heal from within.

What's interesting is that yoga poses have been used as a form of therapy for thousands of years. We all know that physical exercises help us to lose weight, get stronger and increase our muscle mass, but the poses affected by practicing yoga do much more than that. They can help with depression and healing after a divorce.

Since yoga is about mind-body awareness, it's important for us to notice our thoughts during meditation so they can make the experience even better through cognitive restructuring. This means learning how to change negative thoughts into positive ones or just not taking them too seriously when they appear in your mind during your yoga practice.

To get started, you'll need to find a good yoga teacher. I talked about my wonderful online yoga teacher,

Adriene, who is based in Austin, Texas, in chapter 13, Grieving a broken relationship - I recommend that you check out 'Yoga With Adriene' on YouTube for her free online high-quality practices on yoga and mindfulness. You can learn *'asanas'* (body positions and postures) and *'pranayama'* (breath control practices) with Adriene and her most adorable dog, Benji, who is always on screen with her, to set yourself up for greatness and feeling good every day!

Benefits of Yoga during and after a divorce

It offers rest and relaxation in your body, mind and spirit. It's good for people to practice and get into a daily habit because it helps with stress management. The poses help to release tension in the body and muscles so that the mind can let go. Breathing is a great way to calm down the nervous system and mind and will leave you feeling better in no time.

Meditation

Meditation is like a detox for the mind. It is a way to turn your mind off so that you can more easily accept what is happening in your life. The thoughts and feelings will still be there, but they will no longer be a source of frustration.

When we close our eyes, we concentrate on the world inside ourselves. This can be very calming in a stressful situation. Try it for yourself.

There are several stages to meditation, and you can take whatever suits you the best:

1) You should choose a time when you have nothing scheduled for at least five minutes. You will usually be in a

more positive frame of mind right before sleeping or right after waking up.

2) Your breathing should be slow and calm. If it is not, try breathing through your nose while counting to three as you inhale and counting to six as you exhale. Close your eyes, focusing on your breathing and any other sounds that are around you.

3) When you have reached a point where you are in tune with your breathing, and the sounds you hear are not the background noise of an ordinary day, then you should begin to concentrate on your thoughts.

4) At this point, you should be able to relax and become aware of the feelings within your mind. As thoughts come up that are not helpful to your situation, simply breathe through them.

5) When you feel completely at peace, open your eyes and re-evaluate how everything feels. If it still feels like a painful situation, try again over a longer period of time over days or weeks.

You can also practice guided meditations that help you find inner calm and peace to reset your thought patterns to a higher vibration. There are plenty of Apps for this on the market and free guided meditations on YouTube. I currently listen to: *'Be Your Most Powerful Self'* by Jason Stephenson, which is an 8-hour sleep positive affirmations meditation.

Many people also meditate by aligning the seven chakras. A *'chakra'* is an energy centre that is found in the physical body. There are seven main energy centres that align along the spine, starting from the base of the spine to the crown of the head. The chakras are responsible for different aspects of our physical, emotional and spiritual well-being. An easy way to visualise the chakras is as follows:

1) **Root Chakra**: Located at the base of the spine and covers the first three vertebrae, the bladder and the colon; this chakra has a great influence on one's self-esteem and authority within their own life. When this chakra is open, we feel safe, stable, secure and fearless.

2) **Sacral Chakra**: Located in the abdomen, between reproductive organs, this chakra is responsible for health, personal well-being, relationships with others, sexuality and survival instincts.

3) **Solar Plexus Chakra**: Located beneath the waist and above the stomach, this chakra is responsible for personal power, decision-making abilities, self-esteem, and strength of character.

4) **Heart Chakra**: Located in the heart area, this chakra is responsible for the love of others, self and spirit. It is also responsible for forgiveness.

5) **Throat Chakra**: Located in the throat area, this chakra is responsible for creativity, intellect and communication. When this chakra is open, it gives us the ability to speak our highest truths.

6) **Third Eye Chakra**: This chakra is located between the eyebrows and just above your forehead. This chakra is where inspiration, intuition and imagination come together to work as one with intellectual reasoning. It is also responsible for achieving one's spiritual path.

7) **Crown Chakra**: This centre sits on top of the head, the crown. It is where the connection between your

physical and spiritual selves exists. It is what allows you to be in touch with your higher self and, ultimately, to the Divine.

Grounding to Mother Nature

Do you find the smell of soil that has been freshly rained on appealing? There's something innately comforting about that smell. But what about the feel of a leaf or sand between your toes and fingers? Or the sound of a bird chirping in the distance?

Many people are finding that by connecting to Mother Earth, she can help provide balance in their lives.

Strolling barefoot through a lawn is a wonderful way to relax, absorb the earthy smells and enjoy the healing vibes. Whenever you're stressed, go for a walk. You could walk to a nearby park and watch squirrels chase each other. Gaze at the stars on a clear night and listen to the sound of daytime or night-time creatures and other animals. Venture further afield and go for a nature hike, like the Yorkshire three peaks that I did recently with my two sisters. The experience blew me away! Being on and one with the lands, seeing Mother Nature upfront in her full glory, was breathtaking and exhilarating.

Spending time outdoors is an excellent way for us to reconnect with nature. Feeding ducks, taking walks along the seaside, swimming in a lake or river, sitting on the patio watching clouds go by... there is so much to experience with Mother Nature. Just give it a go and see how it transforms your life! You'll find yourself feeling calmer and much more relaxed in no time.

CHAPTER 16:

VISUALISING YOUR FUTURE

The law of attraction is the concept that whatever you pay attention to and focus on you will attract into your life. It has been packaged as a new-age phenomenon, but this philosophy has been around for thousands of years. Buddha's teachings - *"What you think, you become. What you feel, you attract. What you imagine, you create."*

This law is based on the idea that you are not your body, but you are a vibrating energy pattern within a field of energy. So, every decision or thought you have, or literally any thinkable suggestion from your mind, is a request of some kind to the universe.

As we visualise the things that we want, we radiate energy towards them. When we consistently send out the right kind of thoughts and signals, we start to feel drawn to where our thoughts are pointing. We begin to notice that as we continue doing this, more things in our life just start to happen and align as a result of our thought patterns.

It's quite simple, really: You attract what you think about, not what you say or do. Your thoughts become your words and deeds. This is a deep topic, and if you are curious about it, I recommend you consider the work of Esther, and Jerry Hicks, who co-wrote several books together; the most famous ones are: *'The Law of Attraction'* and *'Ask and It is Given.'*

I also suggest you review the work of Dr. Joe Dispenza who has also written multiple books and scientific articles on the mind-body connection and the role and function of the human brain to tap into our true full human potential. His first book, *'Evolve Your Brain: The Science of Changing Your Mind'* is mind-blowing and will be a life changing read!

So, with the above understandings, we can examine our lives and see exactly how our energy, vibrations and frequency have shaped our lives for our benefit and/or detriment.

What is visualisation?

'Visualisation' is the act of imagining something, someone or a particular outcome that you desire in your life, believing in it and rehearsing it as a reality in your mind. Renowned athletes use this technique to create peak performance and to be at the top of their game. However, let's not be naive about it; visualisation alone will not get anyone results - you must take action in line with your goals and objectives.

How can we use it to cope after a divorce?

1. Start by setting intentions and visualising your goals

For us to manifest anything in this world, it is key to focus on what we want to happen rather than what we don't want. If we focus on what we don't want, then we are likely to attract that, as where our focus goes, energy flows in that direction.

By taking the time to set a clear intention at the beginning of each day that you are ready to let go of worry, fear and stress and set intentions for things that you want to come into your life, you will be more likely to be open-minded and receptive.

Try writing all the things that you wish for, whether it be for yourself or others. Then close your eyes and imagine them happening, seeing everything in vivid detail. This is how we bring our desires into reality by using our imagination. By rehearsing the desired goals and outcomes in our minds, just like top athletes do to train to win.

Let's say that we want to meet someone exciting after this divorce is over. By clearly saying to ourselves that we want to meet a new compatible partner and visualising a new love, it will open our minds to receiving new opportunities. We must then make a conscious effort to socialise and be open to new possibilities; they will not manifest on their own!

2. Relax the mind

The next step is to relax the mind so that we can receive what we want. Relaxing and grounding ourselves will help us to listen to our inner voice and our intuition. Here, we imagine that all our worries and fears have melted away, leaving us feeling light and free.

3. Focus on the heart

A powerful way of manifesting your hopes and dreams into reality is through heart-centred practices like loving yourself unconditionally and cultivating self-compassion. For example, if you feel that you have experienced a huge loss after your divorce, it is important not to blame yourself or others for anything. Instead, recognise your feelings without judgment and take responsibility.

4. Repeat positive affirmations

An affirmation refers to a phrase or sentence that is repeated to oneself. This helps to quieten the mind and aids us in focusing on living authentically and in accordance with one's true feelings. It is important to make affirmations that resonate and work for you, so that you can relate better with your inner voice and act accordingly.

Examples of short but positive affirmations include:

"I am fearless and can do anything that I put my mind and body to. I am the master of my mind and destiny!"

"I love and approve of myself, and I know that all is well and as it should be!"

"I trust the process of life and know that the universe has always got my back and is supporting me!"

5. Reaffirm your abilities

Affirmations are a powerful way to help you to believe in yourself and believe that you can make your dreams come true. By making a list of affirmations and repeating them out aloud daily, each time you do this, it will strengthen your belief in your ability to achieve your goals so long as you genuinely believe that you can achieve them.

We become more open as we start sharing what we are thinking about on a regular basis with someone we trust.

Our thoughts slowly transform from an idea or imagination into reality by the law of attraction. Some people may call this *'mirror work'* or *'talk therapy'*. The concepts are similar; you are either affirming in front of a mirror or stating the affirmations out aloud either to yourself or to a trusted confidant. The key to successful visualisation is to follow through with consistent action steps in line with your goals and objectives.

Once we learn to do this, we can attract more positive things into our life. Having a positive attitude will bring you experiences that are of equal or higher vibration. So, the key is to always make a conscious effort to reach for the higher frequencies and vibrations, positive feelings and thoughts.

CHAPTER 17:

MOVING ON TO NEW RELATIONSHIPS

After letting go of the past; we will start to experience new love. A love that is based on a newfound appreciation for ourselves. This will make us feel lighter, happier, and more alive than ever before. We have now learnt to appreciate our own hearts, minds and bodies and understand what we truly want in life. We'll know that the pain of divorce won't last forever and that the best times are still yet to come with our new relationships.

We'll know we're ready for another romantic relationship when we feel it inside. The heart will never lie. If it's right, then we'll know it. So, when you're ready to move on to something more fulfilling, then be open and available to new possibilities!

<u>When should you start dating after a divorce?</u>

While there's no magic formula for when you should start dating again, there are a few unspoken rules that most people abide by.

The first is to wait until after the decision to divorce becomes final. In other words, wait until there is no possibility of reconciling with your ex-spouse.

You need to feel like yourself again and back in control of your life. This can take a lot longer than you think, and it's important not to rush it. Letting go takes time, especially when dealing with an emotional event such as divorce. Moving on to new relationships can be healing and wonderful, but it can also be emotionally draining.

If you're not ready to date yet, then that's okay too. Take the time to reflect on what loss really means to you. What was your relationship like? How did it end? What are your long-term goals and objectives in life? How do you see yourself changing in the future? Once you've healed and re-evaluated who you are today, and you know your core values, then come back later and readjust these ideas of what dating should be like for yourself.

Asking the real questions

Why do you want to date? Are you running away from loneliness? Are you feeling like you're missing out by staying home alone? Are you overcompensating for any self-esteem issues? Lastly, are you doing it because the idea of being with someone new feels scary and scary is better than feeling lonely?

Before you get into a new relationship, it's important to know why you're doing it. Have an honest conversation with yourself and let your feelings out. Be sure to have these conversations with friends, family or your therapist so that you can be sure that this is something that you want and not something that's being projected onto you.

There are also practical questions to ask yourself. What kind of person will make you happy? Do you need a serious relationship? If so, how serious? Are you looking for someone to go on adventures with? Are you looking for someone more laid-back and easy-going?

Think of what you want in the next relationship. Will it be like the past one? How long do you want it to last? How would you define a successful relationship?

Be sure that you're taking the time to think about all these things so that you can be confident in your next choice. If it feels right, then go for it! This is something that shouldn't be taken too seriously when you get back out there on the dating scene. In the early stages, you will be apprehensive and probably a little anxious. But just keep an open mind and have some fun!

<u>The trap in casual hookups</u>

After a divorce, people often feel a sense of freedom that they weren't able to experience while they were married. This can be an exciting and exhilarating time, but it is also important to know where the line is between enjoying yourself and trying too hard to forget your ex-spouse.

When you're looking for a new relationship, it's important to think about what you're really looking for at a deeper level. Are you looking to meet someone? Are you looking for an adventure or some excitement? Do you want something long-term but with no strings attached?

Casual hookups are based on chemistry and not long-term compatibility. Whenever you're looking for a relationship, you have to think about the whole package.

This is why casual hook-ups are not recommended for people who are looking for a long-term authentic relationship.

Putting it all together

In this book, we've learnt that a holistic approach to divorce that comes from a place of love, kindness, compassion, acceptance, understanding, letting go, forgiveness, no judgement and patience will yield the best results for us, our children and future generations by breaking the cycle of dysfunctional and hurt families. It will avoid unnecessary prolonged pain and suffering.

This model is not a silver bullet, and I know it will not work for all families due to extenuating circumstances, but it's one of the most effective strategies that I have practised with clients who choose to work with me. I have also experienced this first-hand in dealing with my own separation and divorce. A holistic approach to divorce is an example of how to sustain collaborative relationships post-separation and divorce. Despite our differences, the result of this approach will be better for everyone involved.

We've seen how divorced couples can co-parent well. We've seen how both parents can push their egos aside and protect their children. It's not just about being nice to each other; it's also about being kind to ourselves. Giving us, our children and future generations the opportunity to move on and lead happier, healthier and more fulfilled lives post-separation and divorce.

What's next?

Now that we know what to do and how to do it, life after divorce can be happier and more fulfilling than it was before. It's a new beginning and chapter for you and your children. It's time to move forward and have fun!

What is the best tip on divorce that you've picked up? I'd love to hear your views. Please leave a review and let me know how your story ends.

It is my sincere wish and desire, that you go on to thrive and lead your best lives moving forwards.

With love and light,

Sushma Kotecha

February 2023

You can contact Sushma via the link below:

https://linktr.ee/Holistic_Family_Mediation

Printed in Great Britain
by Amazon